JUDAISM IN THE NEW
TESTAMENT PERIOD

JUDAISM IN THE NEW TESTAMENT PERIOD

BY

R. TRAVERS HERFORD, B.A.

AUTHOR OF "CHRISTIANITY IN TALMUD AND MIDRASH," "PHARISAISM, ITS
AIM AND ITS METHOD," "THE PHARISEES." EDITOR OF "PIRKE
ABOTH." CONTRIBUTOR TO "THE LEGACY OF ISRAEL,"
AND TO "JEWISH STUDIES IN MEMORY OF
ISRAEL ABRAHAMS," ETC., ETC.

THE LINDSEY PRESS
5, ESSEX STREET, STRAND, LONDON, W.C. 2
1928

PRINTED IN GREAT BRITAIN BY
RICHARD CLAY & SONS, LIMITED,
BUNGAY, SUFFOLK.

PREFACE

This book is intended primarily for those readers of the New Testament who have no knowledge of Hebrew or of the Rabbinical literature. No references have been given to that literature, but the whole of the book is the outcome of the author's study of it during a period of nearly fifty years.

Those readers who wish to know more in detail of the Rabbinical evidence for what is stated in this book will find much of it in the author's books *Christianity in Talmud and Midrash*, 1903 (now out of print), and *The Pharisees*, 1924. And they will find a perfect mine of information in the recent work of Prof. George Foot Moore, *Judaism in the Early Centuries*, 1927, a book which ought entirely to supersede the works of Weber and Bousset, the broken reeds upon which Christian scholars have long been accustomed to lean. They will also find invaluable help in *Studies in Pharisaism and the Gospels*, First and Second Series, by the late Israel Abrahams. Also in Klausner's *Jesus of Nazareth*, of which there is an English translation by Danby.

My cordial thanks are offered to the Managers

of the Lindsey Press for their kindness in undertaking the publication of this book, and thus bringing to the notice of many readers a view of the subject which is not the usual one, but which may be deserving of serious consideration.

R. TRAVERS HERFORD.

Kelsall, Chester,
1928.

CONTENTS

CHAP.   PAGE

I. JUDAISM BEFORE THE PERIOD OF THE NEW
TESTAMENT   9

II. GROWTH OF SECTS AND PARTIES . . .   39

III. THE TEACHING OF THE PHARISEES . .   80

IV. NON-PHARISAIC JUDAISM   119

V. JUDAISM IN OPERATION   140

VI. THE IMPACT OF CHRISTIANITY ON JUDAISM .   183

VII. SEPARATION OF CHRISTIANITY FROM JUDAISM .   222

JUDAISM IN THE
NEW TESTAMENT PERIOD

CHAPTER I

JUDAISM BEFORE THE PERIOD OF THE NEW TESTAMENT

READERS of the New Testament are met, on almost every page, by allusions to Jewish ideas, beliefs and usages. In the three earlier Gospels, the whole atmosphere, so to speak, is Jewish; and, in regard to the New Testament as a whole, if the Jewish element were removed the remainder would be unintelligible. It is obviously, therefore, of the first importance that the reader should have some knowledge of Judaism as it was known and taught and lived during the period covered by the New Testament literature. Nearly all the chief persons concerned in the rise of Christianity were Jews, and much of the teaching contained in the New Testament is more or less closely related to Judaism. Even where it is in sharp conflict with Jewish teaching, the force of the opposition cannot be estimated without a knowledge of the teaching which was opposed. Jesus himself was a Jew, and it does not appear that he ever looked upon himself as having ceased to be such. If he severely criticised the religious teachers of his time, he nevertheless had a good deal in common with them, much more than is usually recognised. And, if this were questioned or denied, it could only be decided on the evidence furnished by a real and independent knowledge of what the Judaism of his time really was, and what its exponents really taught.

It would be generally admitted that such a knowledge of Judaism as is required cannot be obtained from the New Testament itself. Christian scholars have usually drawn upon the writings of the Jewish historian Josephus, and upon certain books classed together under the general title of Apocalyptic literature, books of Jewish origin largely concerned with the expectation of the Messiah, the end of the world and subjects related therewith. Of the Apocalyptic literature more will be said in another connexion. It is only known in Greek or other translations, the Hebrew original text having been lost. Josephus also wrote in Greek ; and thus the whole of the material usually taken for the foundation of a description of Judaism in the New Testament period is such as can be read by a scholar who can read Greek and who cannot read Hebrew, at least not the Hebrew of the period in question. Josephus and the Apocalyptic literature are useful so far as they go ; but they do not go nearly so far as they are commonly supposed to go. Josephus undoubtedly knew a good deal about Judaism ; but he was writing for Roman readers who had not his interest in the subject and were not in a position to check his statements if they had wished to do so. The Apocalyptic literature certainly represents an element in the Judaism of its time, but it was an element of very minor importance compared with those in which lay the real vitality and strength of Judaism. It is a fundamental mistake to suppose that the Apocalyptic literature can explain what Judaism really stood for, in that or any other age. And because Josephus and the Apocalyptic books, taken with the New Testament itself, are practically the only sources from which Christian scholars have drawn their knowledge of Judaism, that knowledge has been usually superficial and defective.

There is, however, another source of information whose importance and value are so great as to put Josephus and the Apocalyptic writers entirely in the shade. This is the Rabbinical literature, contained in a large number of works of which the Talmud is the chief, and whose contents cover a long period including that of the New Testament. All the works comprised in this literature are written in Hebrew or Aramaic, sometimes, especially in the Talmud, extremely difficult, and only a small portion has been translated into English or other modern languages. To scholars who read only Greek and Latin the Rabbinical literature is inaccessible; which is no doubt the reason why Christian scholars have usually ignored it, and thought they had all they needed in the Greek sources mentioned above. But the truth remains that a knowledge of the Rabbinical literature is the only reliable foundation for any description of Judaism as it was in the New Testament period, at least any description which shall be in accordance with the facts. For this literature represents the ideas of those who led the main movement in Judaism, both before and after the rise of Christianity, the men of most influence and creative power as religious teachers. From them and their words can be learned what Judaism really meant to those who best understood it, meant on its own account and not by comparison with any other form of religion. This literature does not cover the whole of Judaism. It was the work of the Pharisees, and Pharisaism was only one out of several component elements in the Judaism of the time. But it gives a picture of Judaism as seen from the inside such as can be found nowhere else; and, though the picture is not complete, the study of it is quite indispensable if any real knowledge is to be obtained of Judaism as it was in the period of the New Testament.

And there is this further, that only through the study of the Rabbinical literature is the remarkable fact disclosed—a fact unsuspected by most students of the Christian origins—that Judaism was hardly at all affected by the rise of Christianity. There was a temporary disturbance, but no appreciable permanent effect. Judaism did change, certainly, during the New Testament period, but it did so for reasons which lay quite apart from Christianity. The war which ended with the fall of the Temple, A.D. 70, and the war which ended with the overthrow of the Messianic leader Bar Cocheba and the destruction of the Jewish state in A.D. 135, had a

profound effect upon the Judaism which survived
them; but Christianity in its rise made hardly any
impression on the Judaism with which it was confronted. Judaism was continuous throughout its
history, changing indeed in the course of centuries,
but not interrupted by any sudden dislocation, and
this applies to the New Testament period. Judaism
was continuous then with what it had been before
and with what it became afterwards, and showed
no special characteristic change due to its passage
through that period. So far as Judaism is concerned, there would be no particular reason for
studying it just in that one period. From the
point of view of Judaism, Christianity when it
appeared was a disturbing factor which soon lost
its force, as its exponents drew away from the circle
of Judaism and passed out into the great Gentile
world. Not until Christianity had begun to exercise imperial power, in and from the fourth century,
was its influence seriously felt upon Judaism. Such
as Judaism would have been if the events recorded
in the New Testament had not taken place, such
on the whole it remained although those events
did take place.

The Judaism, accordingly, which it is the purpose of this book to describe is a Judaism having a
character of its own, principles, ideals and practices
which existed in their own right, as accepted and
developed by the people who held them, out of the
experience which their history had brought them
and the spiritual insight it had enabled them to
acquire. And for this reason the New Testament
does not and cannot represent Judaism as it really

was. Even the very large amount of Jewish teaching and Jewish concepts which found a place in the New Testament was regarded from a point of view which was not that of Judaism; and the frequent polemical references and hostile criticisms indicate not the real character of the Judaism which was encountered, but the reaction to it of those who came up against it. Neither the encounter nor the reaction can be rightly understood without an independent knowledge of that which was encountered.

If the attempt made in this book to supply that independent knowledge be successful, it will throw light upon what the New Testament contains which bears upon Judaism, but it will not be limited to such reference. For there were elements in Judaism which do not become prominent in the New Testament, some indeed which are not mentioned there at all but which belonged essentially to the Judaism of that period, and therefore helped to determine the reaction of its opponents and the sequence of events in which they were concerned.

When looked at from a distance, as is usually the case with non-Jewish students, Judaism appears to be a well-defined and fairly simple system, with a few strongly marked lines of thought and practice capable of easy description, and supposed to be not less easily understood. But, when studied from near at hand, and still more when studied from within, Judaism is seen to be by no means simple. There were many more types than usually appear, many more shades of belief and practice than those which are commonly described. In this sense it is true to say, in the words of Montefiore, that there were " many Judaisms "; and the phrase suggests a useful caution against hasty generalisation, when describing the Judaism of the New Testament period.

It was said above that the Judaism of this period was continuous with what went before and with what came after it. To understand it, therefore, some indication must be given of what the earlier Judaism was, from the time when that name is first correctly applied to the religion of Israel. The event which marks the transition is the Babylonian Captivity, or Exile, 597–586–536 B.C. A large number of people, including the king Jehoiachin, were carried captive to Babylon in 597, and a second deportation larger in number took place in 586 after the capture of Jerusalem by Nebuchadnezzar. This repeated deportation, together with the overthrow of the kingdom of Judah, had the most far-reaching effect upon the political, social and religious condition of those upon whom the crushing blow fell. Politically there was a complete breach with the past. Those who were carried away were prisoners of war in the train of the king of Babylon. Those who came back were subjects of the king of Persia. The former kingdom of Judah was annihilated, and lay derelict during the Exile, a prey to the marauders and spoilers of the tribes upon its borders. The returning captives on their release could set up no kingdom. They were allowed to gain a precarious foothold in Jerusalem and a small district round that their one city, to live there as a feeble community subject to a Persian satrap, to get on as best they could. There was no Jewish kingdom till four centuries had passed since the Return.

But in regard to religion there was no breach with the past. Those who came back brought with them what was essentially the old religion, only so far different as it was seen in the new light of the experience of the Exile. It was the religion of which the prophets and the priests had been the chief exponents, and it was expressed not merely in present belief but in memories and traditions from a far distant past, partly recorded in writing, partly handed down by word of mouth. There was never any question of setting up a new religion. The returning exiles, when they were able, built a new Temple on the site of the old one; but they were careful to restore, on the ancient lines so far as they could, the worship to be offered there. They did this because that was the place which, in their belief, God had chosen of old, and such were the ceremonies and sacrifices which he had prescribed. He had been with their fathers; he had been with themselves during the Exile; he was with them now, unchanged and unchanging.

The chief contents of the religion thus continued after the Exile were, first and foremost, the belief in one only God, the Sole Creator, the Supreme Ruler. The Exile had put an end, once and for all, to any recognition of other gods. The older prophets had denounced idolatry as a danger to the national religion, a disloyalty of which their countrymen might be and often were guilty. After the Exile that danger was no longer present within the community of Israel. Outside the community the danger remained what it always had been, no less but also no greater. Henceforth, the Jew stood apart from the Gentile in the affirmation of a strict monotheism. Judaism, as a religion, was finally purified from the last trace of its former taint of idolatry.

The God of Judaism was worshipped as the one only God, but also as having a special relation to the people of Israel, whom he had chosen from among the other peoples. He and his chosen people were bound to each other by a covenant, made with Abraham and often renewed; and he had given, through Moses, a revelation of his will. He had watched over his people and blessed them; and, because he had chosen them, he punished them when they disobeyed him. They, on their side, were bound by the covenant to serve him; and their past history was the record of how they had succeeded or failed.

The relation between the God of Israel and his people was not merely that of ruler and subject, protector and protected. So much might be claimed by other nations in respect of their own gods. The demand of the God of Israel on his people was a moral demand. " Ye shall be holy for I am holy " is the keynote of Judaism, and has been in all its history. And, whatever may have been the original implications of the word " holy," the development of the religion of Israel has always been towards an ethical ideal, in its conception of God as he is and of man as he ought to be. The Old Testament bears abundant witness to the height which was reached in the ascent towards that ideal. That is

B

the great contribution of the prophets, and that is what made the religion of Israel intrinsically different from all other religions then known. The chief element in the ethical character of the religion of Israel was the conception of God as Just, a conception which is indeed the bedrock of Judaism. To say that the God of the Old Testament religion was a jealous God, a vengeful despot and the like, is only true in regard to some, and those the earlier, stages in the development of that religion, and it is not characteristic of Judaism as distinguished from the other religions amidst which it grew up. The God of the Old Testament religion began, in the belief of those who first worshipped him, as a tribal god like other tribal gods. But, in respect of his power, he became the Almighty; and from being a God of vengeance he became the God of righteousness, holy and just, so that the feeling towards him of those who worshipped him became that of trust, unshakeable confidence, the conviction that to serve him with entire devotion was the whole duty of man. Out of this conception of the relation of God to man, and more especially (in the Old Testament) to Israel, there grew the sense of personal affinity between them; so that it became possible to represent God and Israel under the figure of father and children, and to speak of love from each towards the other. This is what makes the Old Testament so pre-eminently the book of personal religion, quite apart from any interest in the history, legislation or other matter which it contains.

In the contents of the religion of Israel, as it survived the Exile, must be included the ideas of reward and punishment, usually expressed in terms of material prosperity and adversity, and connected with obedience and disobedience towards God. The personal relation between God and Israel gave to the concepts of Sin, Repentance and Forgiveness an intensity and a depth of meaning peculiar to the religion of Israel; and this deeper meaning was recognised and developed alongside of the ritual of sacrifice which expressed the ancient idea of establishing harmony between God and man, and of restoring it when it had been broken. The organised worship of God was carried out fully only in the Temple in Jerusalem, and the priests who officiated there performed their duties on behalf of all the people. The services in the Temple brought to a focus the collective purpose of Israel to adore God, and gave a local meaning to the thought of approach to him. And, while the organised expression of religion was thus chiefly confined to the Temple, the two older institutions of the Sabbath and the rite of circumcision were observed by all Israel in every place.

The religion which those who returned from the Exile brought with them contained no certain trace of a belief in immortality or resurrection; probably no trace at all, only the ancient expectation of a ghostly existence of the dead in Sheol, the underworld. Hope for the future did not extend beyond the earthly life; and the golden age, of which the prophets had spoken, and with which the name of the Messiah was associated, had reference to the community of Israel living on earth at some future time.

Such in mere outline were the chief contents of the religion of Israel, the main concepts in the minds of those who returned from the Exile. To be more precise, these were the elements in the religion of the time before the Exile which were carried into the period that began with the Return.

To these inherited elements were added others which were due to the experience acquired during the Exile, and it is these which mark the difference between the Religion of Israel and Judaism properly so called. The latter grew out of the former, but was not identical with it. The difference consists partly in a change in the emphasis laid upon elements already present in the inherited religion, and partly in the use of new means to meet needs which, if not themselves new, became more urgent than they had formerly been. It is not intended that such change as is here indicated was at once apparent on the return from the Exile. The change was very gradual, and extended over many generations, before its effects were fully seen. What is meant is that after the Exile that which had been the Religion of Israel developed along a certain line and acquired a character to which the name Judaism is properly applied. We have accordingly to consider what were the factors which brought about that change, and the presence of which constitutes that difference.

Judaism after the Exile differed from the religion of the older time in laying increased emphasis upon the individual, in all that concerned religion. Further, it possessed an institution unknown to the older religion, of far-reaching importance, in the Synagogue. Moreover, the individualising of religion was carried out along a line peculiar to Judaism, in the development of the *Torah* *— usually, but quite wrongly, called the Law.

So little is known of the conditions prevailing immediately after the Return, that no answer is possible to the question whether the process of individualising had already begun. The first clear sign of it is not seen till the arrival of Ezra a full century after the end of the Captivity, when it becomes indeed very plain. Up till his time we may suppose that the members of the community in and around Jerusalem did little more than carry on, maintaining their religion without appreciable change on the lines of their inherited usage. Nevertheless, the way had been already prepared, or at least the direction had been pointed out which would lead towards such an individualising of religion as marked the fully developed Judaism. The prophet Ezekiel, during the Exile, had taught a doctrine of individual responsibility which was new in his time, and which, though it might be reconciled with the older teaching of communal solidarity, was by no means identical therewith. What led Ezekiel to that new idea it is impossible to say; but it is at least conceivable that it was one result of the impression made upon him by the sharp discipline of the Exile. That calamity had befallen Israel no doubt as the punishment for the accumulated sins of many generations. " The fathers have eaten sour grapes and the children's

* The term Torah will be explained below, and the reasons given for retaining the Hebrew word untranslated throughout this book. See p. 30.

teeth are set on edge " was an old proverb, which Jeremiah had applied in his time (Jer. xxxi. 29). Ezekiel took up the idea and carried it further. The blow had fallen on the children ; and how could that be just, unless in some way they had themselves deserved it ? There must be, in the scheme of the divine justice, a place and a meaning for the individual, on his own account and not merely as a member of the community or the descendant of a line of ancestors. Whatever the former generations might have done or failed to do, the present generation had its own task, its own responsibility towards God. And if it were the community which had sinned and brought down the punishment of the Exile, the community would not have sinned unless the several members of the community had each a share in that sin. Evidently the way to retrieve the disaster and enter upon a better course for the future was to take serious concern for the individual, and teach him that he must take serious concern for himself, if he would serve God.

During the Exile there was little or no opportunity of putting these ideas into practice, even if they had been consciously formulated. Ezekiel had started them, and presumably they passed into the minds of some of his companions in Exile who heard his teaching. There they germinated, waiting their time and the appearance of some teacher who could give practical application to them under more favourable conditions. That teacher was Ezra, and his time did not arrive until a century had passed since the first return from Babylonia.

But during the Exile the first beginning was made of an institution which was destined to play a part of quite immeasurable importance in the history not only of Judaism but also of Christianity. This was the Synagogue, which became the central institution in Judaism and the parent not of Christianity but of the Christian Church as an institution.

It is generally agreed that the beginning of the Synagogue must be placed in the period of the Exile; not because there is any direct evidence of the fact, but because no later time can be found when the conditions were present which would most naturally account for its origin. It is true that the Synagogue as a definite institution does not make any certain appearance till long after the Exile; but it must have had a beginning some time, and there is nothing to make it probable, still less certain, that it was invented and set going in the complete form which it wears when it first emerges into clear view.

The essence of the Synagogue is congregational worship and edification, conducted by the congregation through their own members, not by priests on their behalf, and laid out on lines necessarily quite different from those appropriate to the Temple services. A building set apart for such congregational meeting was not indispensable, though usually convenient and generally made use of from the time when the Synagogue became a well-established institution. But, in any case, the building was not, like the Temple, restricted to one special place; it could be erected anywhere and in any number according to the requirements of Jews wherever they happened to be, and to whatever distant land they might have found their way.

To understand, therefore, how the Synagogue first came into being, it is not necessary to assume anything more than the occasional meeting of a few of the exiles in small groups here and there for mutual encouragement and consolation. They were cut off from the homeland, and there was no longer the Temple to draw their thoughts and aspirations as the focus of their religion. Whether any provision had been made for communal worship apart from the Temple in the days before the Exile is not known; but there was certainly the need of it in Babylonia, and, if religion were not to be allowed to die out altogether, the captives must themselves provide the means for preserving it. That they were in a position to make any collective effort for this purpose there is nothing to show, and it is not necessary nor warrantable to assume such a collective effort. But it may very well have happened that someone here and there gathered a few neighbours together, and that they reminded one another of the truths of their religion, prayed to God who was with them in their foreign land, and called to mind his promises and his mercies to their fathers. Some priest might be able to read to them from the older sacred writings, and, out of a fuller knowledge of the past, might give them help for the present need and hope for the future. Such occasional meetings would be repeated because they met a real want, and the example they set would be followed by others here and there for the same reason. On the lines here suggested there was no idea of inventing a new institution, let alone of imitating on a small scale what had been done in the Temple. Anything of that kind was entirely out of the question. The Temple and all connected with it belonged to Jerusalem alone and could not be reproduced anywhere else. Among the captives in Babylon there was, in greater or less degree, the conscious need of what is implied in worship and service of God, and they took the simplest and most direct way of supplying that need. If they had not done so their religion would have died out, or they would have transferred their allegiance to the gods of Babylon, which would have amounted to much the same thing. That their religion did not die out goes without saying. There was sufficient vitality in it to survive the Exile and to grow into the Judaism known to history. In like manner with regard to the origin of the Synagogue. No matter how simple may have been its first beginnings (and they cannot well have been simpler than what has been suggested above), there must have been sufficient vitality in the practice of religious meetings to enable it to be transplanted to the homeland by the returning exiles. The Synagogue certainly did make its appearance in Palestine at some time. It seems more probable that it began in Babylonia during the Exile, when some provision had of necessity to be made for the maintenance of religion, than that it began after the Return and the rebuilding of the Temple, when there was at least as much provision for the maintenance of religion as there had been before the Exile.

This being granted, then it may be conceded that the development from the original casual meeting for worship and edification into the Synagogue known to history was very gradual. It would seem likely that the first elements to become fixed were the custom of meeting regularly on the Sabbath and that of reading from the Scriptures to the persons assembled. The earliest traces of a rudimentary liturgy may perhaps be assigned to a time not long after Ezra. Even in the period of the New Testament very little was in existence of the liturgy as it is known now. But the fact of importance is that from the time of the Return from the Exile there was effectively established the practice of periodical meetings for worship and religious instruction, entirely independent of priesthood, ritual, sacrifice, or special locality. Any group of persons desiring this simpler form of worship could set it up in any place, and, if their means allowed, could provide a building in which to meet, and whatever else tended to secure its permanent existence. In this way Synagogues came to be a regular feature in the life of Jews wherever they might be, so many centres of religious influence planted in the towns and villages and near to the dwelling of every Jew. When the Synagogue was fully established there was nothing like it in connexion with any form of religion then known; and there has been nothing like it ever since, except its two descendants the Christian Church and the Mohammedan Mosque. To have created the Synagogue is perhaps the greatest practical achievement of the Jews in all their history.

By the time the New Testament period is reached the Synagogue was an institution known to be ancient, and there were Synagogues in every considerable Jewish centre of population, not only in Judæa and Galilee, but also in the chief towns and cities of those countries of the then known world where Jews were to be found. In all of them regular meetings were held for congregational worship, and not for worship only, but also for study and instruction in the Torah. The Synagogue has never in all its history been exclusively a place of worship. It has always been a centre and source of religious influence, a place where the needs of the soul in relation to God and man could find their fullest satisfaction, partly through worship and partly through instruction. When the Synagogue is mentioned in the New Testament, such is the character of the institution, and such the part it played in the life of the people.

Now the Temple had been rebuilt shortly after the Return from the Exile, and again by Herod just before the New Testament period begins. During four centuries at least, the Temple and the Synagogue had existed side by side; and this fact, whose importance is by no means generally recognised, suggests the question What was the relative influence of each in the life of the Jewish people, more especially in the New Testament period? The Temple was, of course, a great national institution, the one and only seat of the ancient ritual and sacrificial worship, the place most closely associated with the God of Israel. The Temple in its splendour was the glory of the Jewish people, their pride and their delight; and, while it stood, there was nothing to rival it on its own domain. Nevertheless, in the day to day, year in year out religious life of the people, the Synagogue counted for much more than the Temple did. Apart from the inhabitants of Jerusalem, the Jewish population visited the Temple only three times a year; and, when they did go there, they looked on at an elaborate ritual service performed by the priests, in which they themselves had little or no active share. No doubt they felt a very deep concern for the performance of the service in the right way and with due magnificence, for it was the collective act of the whole people, expressing its desire to obey the divine will by such ceremonies and such agents as were specified in the Scripture and hallowed by ancient usage.

But all this did not come closely home to them in their daily life in the same way or to the same extent that the Synagogue did. That was, so to speak, at their doorstep; and regular or only occasional attendance there accustomed them to a form of worship widely different from that of the Temple, and one in which every individual worshipper had a personal concern as great and as immediate as that of any of his neighbours. In that simple service there was prayer, congregational and private, there was reading of the Scriptures, and often an expository address; but there was no sacrifice and next to no ritual. There was no one who held a position corresponding to that of a modern clergyman or minister; and, if a priest happened to be present in the Synagogue, he had no special privilege there except to be called first to the reading of the Torah and to pronounce a special benediction if it were required. It cannot be too strongly insisted on that the religion of the Synagogue was never at any time, from its origin to the present day, a priestly religion. Priests, as priests, had nothing whatever to do with it. Their place and office were in the Temple and nowhere else. Sacrifice of course there could not be in the Synagogue; but the whole idea of sacrifice was entirely absent, and whatever has been the influence of the Synagogue in developing personal piety and individual concern for religion, that influence was exerted in ways and towards ends with which the Temple had nothing to do. Within the New Testament period the Temple was destroyed, A.D. 70, and the whole system of sacrifice, ritual and priesthood associated with it was swept away.

But the Synagogue survived; and the religion which had been fostered in the Synagogue for some six centuries suffered no injury through the fall of the Temple. The Jewish people grieved over the loss of the Temple, but they immediately realised that they could do without it. They have never at any time, then or since, dreamed of doing without the Synagogue. Temple and Synagogue represented two entirely different ideas. The Temple was rooted in the past, and what was done there had grown out of ancient beliefs and practices similar to those found in other religions in their early stages. The Synagogue began at a date comparatively recent, with ideas quite other than those of primitive religion, as to the relation between

God and man; and from the time when the Synagogue first appeared, the passing away of the Temple was a foregone conclusion, though centuries elapsed before the end was reached. The presence of a Synagogue in the precincts of the Temple itself, for probably 150 years before it fell, might even be looked on as a sort of warning held up before the older institution that it would eventually have to give way to the younger. Whether or not this thought was ever consciously present to the minds of any contemporary thinkers and teachers, the fact remains that during the whole of the New Testament period the Synagogue and not the Temple was the chief factor in moulding the Judaism of the people.

Of the type of religion developed in and by the Synagogue more will be said when we have learned to understand another factor, referred to above, which helped to shape the Judaism of the centuries after the Exile. This was the influence of what is properly called the Torah; and the man who virtually created that influence and made it of paramount importance for the Judaism of all succeeding time was Ezra.

Torah is the Hebrew word which is usually, persistently and quite wrongly translated into English by the word Law, in such phrases as The Law, The Law of Moses, the burden of the Law, and a multitude of others, commonly used by non-Jewish writers and preachers when referring to Judaism and criticising what they regard as its shortcomings. Such references, however well meant, miss the whole point; for Torah does not mean

Law, and never did, and the example of Paul, who did most to perpetuate the mischievous error, does not justify either himself or those who have imitated him. Torah means Teaching, at first any kind of teaching given by anyone to anyone else, but more particularly teaching given by God to man through the agency of priest or prophet. The revelation, *par excellence*, was the teaching given to Moses and recorded in the five books ascribed to him, the books commonly referred to as the Pentateuch. In Jewish usage these five books were and still are known by the collective name of the Torah. This alone shows that Torah is wrongly translated by " Law," because there is a great deal in the Pentateuch which is not law at all. But the word Torah, though it always retained its meaning as the name of the five books of Moses, gradually came to be applied to the revelation contained in those books, the whole of what God had imparted of knowledge concerning himself and his will; in short, religion generally as received and apprehended in Jewish minds. It was all Torah, divine Teaching, but the common Hebrew word still used to designate it was made to bear a quite special and comprehensive meaning. It became, so to speak, a technical term in Judaism, such as could not be and certainly was not replaced by any other. Therefore, throughout the present book the word Torah is intentionally left untranslated. And it would be a great gain, as well as a first essential step towards the understanding of Judaism, if all who write or speak on the subject would always use the word Torah, and would regard as a sign of ignorance the continued use of the word " Law " as its supposed equivalent. Unless this point is clearly grasped and constantly borne in mind, it is hopeless to think of understanding Judaism.

It was remarked above that the difference between the Jewish religion as it was before the Exile and as it became after the Return consisted partly in a change of emphasis laid upon what had already been present in the earlier religion. The Torah is the most important instance of this. The idea of divine teaching was deeply rooted in the older religion, not merely in connexion with the revelation made known through Moses, but as teaching given by the priests from time to time to those who came to them for counsel or direction. So too the prophets had declared the word of the Lord as it was revealed to them, and what they proclaimed was obviously part of the divine teaching, in other words Torah. Such ideas were familiar to those who returned from the Exile, but not more prominently than they had been in the older times. The man who first laid special stress on the idea of Torah, and took the first step in the process of raising it to the supreme place it has ever since held in Judaism, was Ezra. He was in a real sense the true founder of Judaism, because he impressed on the older religion the peculiar mark by which Judaism differs from that older religion while still being continuous with it. Ezra followed the lead of Ezekiel in the individualising of religion, in the sense that he insisted on the personal concern of each member of the community for being and doing what God required. Responsibility towards

God rested not only upon all but upon each. The true service of God was not rendered through collective acts done on behalf of the community by consecrated priests, at least it was not rendered only through such acts. It called for the personal action of every separate member of the community according to the circumstances of his individual life. If God had said " Ye shall be holy for I am holy," he had said that to every man in his own conscience, and every man had to answer him there. Ezekiel had represented God as saying, " Son of man, stand upon thy feet, and I will speak to thee."

The teaching of Ezekiel in regard to the individualising of religion had waited till the time should come when someone should be able to apply it and put it into practice. Ezra was the one to do this, and the instrument which he used for the purpose was the Torah. When he came up from Babylon, he brought with him the Book of the Torah of Moses, which may mean either the Pentateuch substantially as we have it now or only the Priestly Code, but in any case all that Ezra regarded as divine teaching given to Moses and by him imparted to his people. This book he read in the most public and solemn manner, so that all might know what it was which God had taught his people, and so that everyone who heard might take it to heart. For each one had his own individual responsibility for the fulfilment of what God required, so far as it applied to himself. The Torah had been given to all Israel, as the ancient covenant had been made at Sinai with all Israel and not the priests

c

alone. What was taught must be learned, taken to heart and obeyed, by every member of the community. The Torah must be owned and accepted as the supreme authority in all that belonged to the right conduct of life by each one who, as a member of the community, claimed a share in the covenant. In the olden time the Torah had been in existence, there had been divine teaching, but it had been disregarded and left unfulfilled. Now, there must be an end of such neglect. What had been taught must be learned; what was commanded must be done; what was obscure, either in teaching or precept, must be made clear, so that the end might be attained for the sake of which the teaching had been given.

The book which bears the name of Ezra, and which contains nearly all that is known about him, shows that he met with much opposition in carrying out his policy. This was only to be expected, because, if the Torah was to be henceforward the supreme authority for the community and for each member of it, then the relations between Jews and non-Jews would have to be very different from those which Ezra found in operation when he came up from Babylon to Jerusalem. Mixed marriages were distinctly forbidden in the Torah (Deut. vii. 3). Therefore such marriages if already made must be dissolved, and Ezra made this drastic measure the first step in his policy of reform. The general result of his policy was to draw a sharp line of division between Jew and Gentile, and to make for the Jewish community a sort of enclosure in the midst of the Gentile world. This was certainly the result of his policy and may perhaps have been his deliberate intention; but it was only the inevitable consequence of raising the Torah to the position of supreme authority. For if the precepts of the Torah were strictly enforced and obeyed, as in regard to the dietary laws, mixed marriages, clean and unclean and so forth, then the separation of Jew from Gentile was thereby already effected. Now Ezra's one ruling idea was to enforce strict obedience to the precepts of the Torah without exception. The various restrictions and prohibitions which, from Ezra's time onwards, prevented assimilation between Jew and Gentile, were not of his invention. They were of unknown antiquity, only until his time they had not been rigorously enforced. Thus, the Judaism which acquired its peculiar character from him was continuous with the religion of the older time; and its peculiar character was due to the fact that he singled out one element, viz. the Torah, and laid upon that one element a stress which had never before been laid upon it. And he did this because by so doing he could bring religion home to the conscience of every member of the community as it had never been brought before.

This is the real significance of the work of Ezra; and to say, as is said by many, that his chief interest lay in the development of the priestly system is to miss the whole point of what he did. If that had been all, there might as well have been no Ezra. There were plenty who could see to it that the Temple and the priesthood were attended to; but it took all the energy of a great man, a great leader, and perhaps a great saint, to stamp upon the religion of his time the mark which all the succeeding centuries down to our own have never effaced.

In spite of the opposition which he met with, Ezra succeeded, by the help of Nehemiah, the governor, in carrying out his policy, and it was ratified and accepted at the great assembly described in Neh. ix. x. No doubt opponents still remained, but on the whole, and within the community, the chief end was secured—that the Torah as contained in the five books of Moses was raised to the position of supreme authority, the sole source of revealed knowledge concerning God, his nature and his will. Every son of Israel who claimed a share in the covenant must henceforth take account of the Torah, and order his life accordingly or neglect it at his own risk.

The necessity made itself felt at once of explaining the Torah so that its teaching might be understood and its precepts made practicable. Cases of conduct arose which were not provided for in the Torah, or on which its directions were uncertain. From the very first, therefore, there were those who made it their business to study the Torah and interpret it. Quite possibly Ezra himself did this, for he is called "the Priest, the Scribe." It had been from time immemorial the function of the priests to give counsel and direction on religious matters to those in need of them, so that Ezra would naturally discharge that duty. That he was also called the Scribe means that there was applied to him the name borne by those who made it their special business to study and interpret the Torah, from the time of Ezra onwards. The Scribes denote in the first instance those who followed his lead in giving practical application to his idea of the supremacy of the Torah. Collectively, the Scribes of the period after his time for several generations were known under the name of the Great Synagogue. To them is due the working out of the policy of Ezra, so that the Torah really was established effectively as the chief corner-stone of Judaism, a fact of which the reality and the importance were not denied by any one, whatever his own loyalty to the Torah might be. Through the Synagogues the influence of the Torah made itself felt, more or less, upon the rank and file of the people; and when the attempt was made by Antiochus Epiphanes in 167 B.C. to impose upon the Jewish people the ideas and practices of the Greek religion and the Greek culture, the result was the revolt led by the Maccabees, which ended in the rout of Hellenism and the final victory of the Torah and the religion based upon it. The political and social consequences of the Maccabean victory cannot be so simply described; but our present concern is with the religion of the people who made, under the Maccabean leaders, their emphatic and decisive reply to the challenge of Hellenism. From that time onwards, the Torah neither feared nor would endure any rival. Judaism had arrived at a complete consciousness of itself and its own distinctive character, as strongly marked off from and vehemently opposed to any and every form of Gentile religion.

No account has as yet been taken of any differences of type within Judaism as a whole. The aim so far has been to show how Judaism, as it was developed after the Exile, was continuous with the religion of Israel before the Exile, and how the difference was due mainly to a change of emphasis laid upon a factor or factors already present in the older religion. That change began with the lead which Ezekiel had given towards the individualising of religion, it was greatly helped by the entirely new institution of the Synagogue, and it was finally realised in the supreme position assigned to the Torah. These three main factors mark the chief difference between Judaism and the older religion. How they were applied and to what different results they led will best be shown by a study of the different forms which Judaism assumed, and which are distinguished by such names as Pharisee, Sadducee and others less familiar. In the following chapter these will be studied in succession, and the details supplied which were necessarily omitted in the foregoing attempt to describe the character of Judaism as a whole.

CHAPTER II

THE Judaism which at the time of the return from the Exile had been, so far as can be discerned, of one general type and of the character indicated in the last chapter, retained that uniformity till after the time of Ezra. For, though his teaching and especially his insistence on the supreme importance of the Torah contained implicitly the seeds of future change and division, yet those seeds took a long time to germinate. When the period of the New Testament is reached, four centuries after the time of Ezra, Judaism is seen to have lost its uniform character, and is represented by several types bearing distinctive names. Some of these are familiar to the reader of the New Testament, others are not named there but are well known from other sources. And, while the several types can be clearly distinguished, the dividing lines are not always so sharply drawn but that one class shades off with another, so that minor types can be distinguished, having some affinity with one or other of the main types. While, nevertheless, all are included within the meaning of Judaism. If it were possible to analyse the Judaism of the New Testament period into all its component elements, the result of the process would be to show how complex a variety is summed up under that

name, and how far from the truth it is to speak of
" the Jews " collectively as if they were all alike, in
respect of their Judaism.   They are, indeed, all akin
to each other ; and it is not difficult to show how
there came to be this variety of types, and what
especial feature distinguished at all events the chief
amongst them.   To do this will be the subject of
the present chapter ; and the method of historical
development will lead to a far more accurate understanding of the significance of each type than the
method of successive description usually followed,
which deals with Pharisees, Sadducees and the rest
one after the other, and gives what are supposed to
be the peculiar characteristics of each.   The latter
method only produces a detailed catalogue, which
does not imply in the writer and does not convey to
the reader any real understanding of the true meaning of the things enumerated.

In the New Testament period the population of
Palestine included the following classes of persons :—
1. Gentiles of various kinds, Syrians, Greeks,
Romans and what not, also Samaritans, who were
neither Jews nor wholly Gentiles.   2. The mass of
the Jewish people not otherwise specified by a distinctive name.   3. Pharisees.   4. Sadducees.   5.
Essenes.   6. Zealots.   7. Herodians.   8. Proselytes.   Outside Palestine, in what is known as the
Diaspora, or Dispersion, Jews and Proselytes were
to be found in most countries of the then known
world, notably in Egypt and in Babylonia.   And
while the Judaism of Egypt shows marked differences from the Judaism of Palestine, to judge by the
Hellenistic literature which is mainly Alexandrian,

yet in the Diaspora as a whole it is probable that the affinity of its type of Judaism was mainly with the Pharisaic type, because Judaism in the Diaspora was propagated chiefly through the Synagogue, which was entirely Pharisaic.

The names above enumerated are, so far, mere names, and it has to be shown how they came to be recognised or adopted as the distinguishing titles of those to whom they are applied. For this purpose it is necessary to take up again the work of Ezra at the point where it was left in the last chapter, and unfold the results which followed from it.

Ezra left, as his legacy to his people, the Torah as the supreme authority in religion, the sole source of revelation, and the duty of obeying the will of God as therein made known and of taking to heart the teaching therein contained. The task of giving instruction to the people in regard to their religious duties had been, from time immemorial, discharged by the priests, and no change in this respect was made by Ezra or for some time afterwards. Some Levites were probably associated with the work, but no laymen. But the fact that the Torah was now the supreme authority made the task of giving religious instruction somewhat different from what it had been before. The Torah, as recorded in the five books of Moses, contained, it is true, many explicit directions to do this and that; but it did not provide for all cases which arose, and what it did enjoin was sometimes incomplete. Religious instruction by the priests must therefore supply what was wanting, as occasion required from time to time. In any given case, the priests directed that such and such an act should be done; and these directions were called *gĕzēroth*, ordinances. The priests gave them because they were authorised to do so in the Torah itself (Deut. xvii. 9–11), and they did not claim that their ordinances were themselves part of the Torah. They were not to be found in the written text; they were authorised supplements to what Moses had written, intended to carry out his purpose in regard to cases which he had not dealt with.

This was the most obvious and natural way of dealing with the problem created by Ezra's policy of making the Torah supreme; but it gradually led to a result which had not been expected. As the ordinances became more numerous, the occasions on which the precepts written in the Torah could be literally obeyed became relatively fewer, so that the Torah tended to become obsolete, a relic of antiquity, venerable indeed but not effective as a present guide to duty. The real, though not the nominal, authority was in process of being slowly transferred from the Torah to the ordinances, from the Book which contained what was meant for all Israel to the priests who were only a part of Israel. How early this tendency was recognised it is impossible to say, but it was recognised, and gradually another conception of the Torah was developed having for its object to make the Torah once more really effective, as Ezra had meant it to be, as a guide to the doing of the will of God by all the people to whom the Torah had been given. The ordinances of the priests had enjoined the doing of certain acts as a religious duty, but the ordinances were not part of the Torah. The obedience to which the people, through their representatives, had pledged themselves at the great assembly described in the book of Nehemiah (Neh. ix. x.) was promised to the Torah as written, and was limited to what was there set down. The things commanded in the ordinances were not to be found there. They rested on the authority of the priests alone. Now no one denied that the things commanded in the ordinances were such as ought to be done, being, as may be supposed, in accordance with ancient custom and general religious usage. But the view was put forth that the real sanction of these things must be contained in the Torah and not in any other authority, and that the priests were not the only persons competent to declare the meaning of the Torah. It was true that the written text did not contain the precepts which were embodied in the ordinances; but, as these were based on ancient usage, there must be a tradition—unwritten— showing how the written text must be interpreted so as to include as part of its true meaning and content the substance of the ordinances. The Torah thus comprised the written text and the unwritten tradition; and both together, not the written text alone, contained the revelation which God had given to Moses and through Moses to all Israel. The obedience to which the whole people had, through their representatives, pledged themselves in the time of Nehemiah, was obedience to the whole Torah thus conceived, the written and the unwritten.

The effect of this new theory was to stop the process by which the Torah was gradually being turned into an archaic relic, and to restore it to its former position as an effective source of religious guidance and instruction. Because the way was open for the fresh thought of the present to interpret the written word of the past, and keep it from becoming petrified. And, if the priests looked with disfavour upon this new way of interpreting the Torah, they were not the only persons who had the right to declare the real meaning of the Torah. If a layman, neither priest nor levite, proved himself able to interpret the Torah, he had as good a right to do so as any priest; for the Torah had been given to all Israel and not to the priests alone. To ask whether in actual fact there was an unwritten Torah, a tradition derived, like the written Torah, from Moses himself, is a question of very small importance for the purpose of the present book. What really matters is that this conception of the unwritten Torah proved to be the means of saving Judaism from decay, and provided the form under which it maintained and developed the extraordinary vitality which has distinguished it down to the present day. And the reason why this conception of the unwritten tradition, making with the written text the true Torah, was of such immense value to Judaism as it proved to be, was that it re-captured the idea of a living religion and an inexhaustible revelation; it taught the Jew that the God whom he worshipped had not only declared his will in words written down in ancient times, but still made known his will in every age to those who sought to do it, by the agency of teachers who could rightly declare the true meaning of the ancient record, as interpreted in the light of their own religious and moral experience. It taught the Jew to realise his own relation to the living God, his " very present help," his " light and his salvation."

At what period this reaction, against the deadening influence of the priestly ordinances through the restriction of the Torah to the written text alone, became articulate cannot be definitely stated. Probably it had much to do with the deep personal piety which found expression in many of the Psalms ; and those who are called in the 1st Book of Maccabees by the name of Assideans (*Hasidim*, pious ones) are evidently connected with this same reaction, this renewed emphasis on living religion and the service of the living God. For the Assideans were those who, in the Maccabean revolt, stood for a purely religious ideal, as distinguished from those who united to their religious zeal a fervent aspiration for political freedom. All were of one mind in defending their religion against the attempts of Antiochus Epiphanes to replace it by a heathen cult ; but the distinguishing name *Hasidim* was given only to those who were exceptional in their devotion to religion pure and undefiled by more worldly policy.

The Maccabean revolt succeeded in attaining both the religious and the political ends in view. Henceforth the religion whose foundation was the Torah was secure from all attacks, and the heads of the Maccabean family were able to establish themselves as rulers of what came to be recognised as a kingdom. The Assideans, Hasidim, are no more heard of under that name ; but the ideal for which they stood was not left without its defenders. Again the conception of the unwritten tradition as an integral part of the Torah along with the written text found its exponents, also its opponents, and both of these bore names which have become famous. For the former are the Pharisees and the latter are the Sadducees.

Neither of these names has reference to the real ground of difference between them, nor indeed is it certain what the names did refer to. But it is certain that the question on which they took opposite sides was the question of the validity of the unwritten tradition as the complement of the written text of the Torah. There were other points of belief and practice, in respect of which the Judaism of a Pharisee differed considerably from the Judaism of a Sadducee; but they are of secondary importance in comparison with the one fundamental difference just described. As for the two names, that of the Pharisees means the " Separated," and it is first mentioned in connexion with an incident which took place in or shortly before the year 106 B.C., when the breach between Pharisees and Sadducees was openly avowed. The name Pharisee may have been given by the opponents or adopted by themselves; but it had no reference to the dispute with the Sadducees. It really denoted those who *separated* themselves from the rank and file of Jews by the observance of strict rules of clean and unclean, tithes, offerings, and the like, and who formed themselves into societies for the better accomplishment of their purpose. The only reason for taking this course would be the desire to carry out as thoroughly as possible the divine will as revealed in the Torah, to make their own lives conform as closely as possible to the religion founded on the Torah, the religion which consisted in devoted service of the living God, owned to be personal and present, and not the mere performance of ceremonial acts prescribed in an ancient text. The men who followed this course of devoted personal service have acquired, through an accident of history, the name of Pharisee. They might have acquired some other name, and it would not have greatly mattered. What does matter is that the men who bore the name were those who were most intent on bringing the religion of Torah to bear on their own lives and the lives of all whom they could influence. They took up and developed to its utmost extent the idea of the Torah as the full and inexhaustible revelation of the will and nature of God; and religion, for them, was the realisation in thought and in act of all that the Torah revealed, so far as it was given to them to apprehend its meaning. This is the central principle of Pharisaism as disclosed in its own literature, which records the words of its own acknowledged leaders and teachers; and the truth of this statement is not altered by the fact that the central principle was developed along lines which are unfamiliar to non-Jewish minds, and led to results which for that reason are seldom rightly judged, but often misunderstood.

The name Sadducee, in like manner, is of uncertain origin. It is usually derived from the name of Zadok, the High Priest in Solomon's time, and is taken to be a sort of general title for the party to which the priests, at all events the more influential priests, belonged. This may be correct, but not all priests were Sadducees and not all Sadducees were priests. Still, there was some general affinity between priests and Sadducees, as is shown in the New Testament (Acts v. 17); and, however the name may have been acquired, the priests would be, of all men, the least likely to look with favour upon the theory which threw the Torah open to all, and took from themselves their ancient privilege of declaring to the people their religious duties. As this theory was based upon the assumption of an unwritten tradition, it was only natural that the priests as a body should repudiate it; or, to put it differently, that the opposition to the new view should find its main support amongst those who stood to lose by its acceptance.

Now there were priests long before there were Pharisees; and the question of the unwritten tradition which formed the ground of opposition between them was not first raised by the priests, nor did it hold so large a place in their interest and their attention as it did in those of the Pharisees. The priests were charged with the due performance of the Temple ritual, the chief expression, and until the rise of the Synagogue the only expression, of the nation's desire to worship. The task was grave and splendid; and, if it did not protect those who discharged it from the temptations which beset every priesthood, it allowed room for real and sincere piety on the part of those who filled the sacred office. Moreover, the High Priest and the more eminent of his colleagues were closely associated with the government of the country, took a prominent part in public affairs, and had to consider questions of policy affecting the relations of Israel with its Gentile neighbours—Syria, Egypt and Rome. They were not a political party, but they necessarily had a good deal to do with politics. Probably they regarded themselves as the real guardians of the true interests of Israel, maintaining its religion on the safe and long-established lines, while not neglecting to strengthen its worldly position. They would find their natural associates in the secular nobility, the heads of great families, the rich and influential men with a considerable stake in the country. The name Sadducee, however it may have come into use, denotes those who held such a position as the one just indicated and looked upon life from such a point of view.

It is evident that men holding such ideas would not welcome any view of the Torah which would enlarge its scope and intensify the strictness of its application to life. The Sadducees, like all other Jews, accepted the Torah, and were entirely sincere in their allegiance to it. But they restricted their allegiance to the written text, as they had a perfect right to do. What was there set down they owned to be binding on them; and, because a good deal of what seemed to be plainly required was not set down there, they were conscious of no disloyalty if they acted according to their own judgment. The Torah, for them, belonged more and more to the past and less and less to the present; and they felt themselves justified, as men of affairs, in acting for the present needs of their country in ways which had no close relation to anything laid down in the Torah. The new view of the Torah, introduced, or revived and developed, by the Pharisees would seem to them

D

an annoying innovation, of no great importance in itself and without any sort of warrant from common sense or recognised authority, but yet capable of doing much mischief if it should come to be widely held. It would seem that the attitude of the Sadducees towards the new teaching was mainly negative, a rejection of its claim, a denial of its affirmations, rather than an attempt to overthrow it by positive argument. The Sadducees were satisfied to keep to the old ways, and probably included amongst their number many exemplary men, sincere in their religion, with a strict sense of duty, in every way respectable, in spite of the fact that their worldly interest led them in the same direction as the principles of their religion. That the Sadducees denied the doctrine of a future life, and the belief in angels and spirits, is in keeping with the general position just described; and that they were strict and even harsh in their legal decisions, as compared with the Pharisees, is the natural result of their adherence to the written text of the Torah, and their repudiation of the unwritten tradition by which the severity of the precepts contained in the Torah was modified in a humaner sense by their opponents.

If the Sadducees, while loyally accepting the Torah, yet tended to minimise its importance not only in theory but still more in practice, the Pharisees made the Torah the very corner-stone of their religious belief and teaching, and exalted its importance in every way. Why they did this has already been shown. It was for them the sole source of revelation, the one means by which religion could be kept fresh and living, the one and only form under which they could conceive of religion at all. How they developed their theory in practice has now to be shown. The contents of the written Torah, the Pentateuch, were partly preceptive, partly narrative; but all were what God had revealed. All therefore must be taken to heart and applied, so that the divine purpose for which the Torah had been given might be fulfilled. This could not be done unless those to whom the Torah had been given understood what was taught therein, so that they could obey the precepts and receive the truth. The Torah must accordingly be interpreted, its meaning must be explained and declared. This was necessary, if only because the written Torah did not provide sufficient guidance, sometimes no guidance at all, for particular cases where action was required as a religious duty. But there was another and a deeper reason. The revelation contained in the Torah was meant for all Israel; and not only for the Israel who received it from Moses, but for the Israel of every generation since. The question which the interpreter had to answer was not " What did the Torah mean when it was first made known ? " but " What does it mean for me now and for those who are living in this present time ? " This distinction is the key to the whole theory of interpretation, as practised by the Pharisees and their successors the Rabbis; for the whole of the Rabbinical literature, at all events down to the Middle Ages, is in form nothing else but interpretation of the Torah. The modern student, of the Bible or any other ancient text, makes it his aim to ascertain, as clearly as possible, what the ancient writer said and what lesson he intended to convey to his readers, under the conditions of that particular time and country in which he lived. The student may draw his own conclusions from what he reads, but he will observe that the conditions under which the ancient writer lived were very different from those of the present day, and that what was " said to them of old " does not always, still less obviously, apply to himself and the people of his time. The Pharisees in their interpretation of Torah were not concerned with the question " What was its meaning for the people who were present at Sinai ? " but with the question " What is its meaning for us now ? " They expressed this by saying that every Jew, in any age, ought to look on himself as having been ideally present at Sinai, when the Torah was given. Which only means that through the Torah the living God speaks to the living soul throughout the ages, to those at least who are able and prepared to listen to the divine teaching. Interpretation, therefore, was the prime necessity in the religion of Torah, or rather the indispensable means of making that religion effective; and the beginnings of it may perhaps be traced back to Ezra (see Neh. viii. 8).

Interpretation of Torah followed two main lines, according as it was applied to the preceptive or to the non-preceptive parts of the written text; and the results obtained along those lines were different in form and distinguished by separate names. The Torah contained the revelation of the will of God and of truth concerning him. If the revelation were not to be in vain, it was evidently the duty of the Jew to do what God willed that he should do. This before anything and everything else. He might not be able to receive the truths revealed; and even if he did, he only *received* them, with more or less of understanding and assent. But, in regard to the will of God, he either did it or did not do it; and his act, in doing what was commanded, was a sort of expression of himself, a realisation of his personality, the definite exercise of his will; it was his own mark impressed on the universe at a given moment. Probably the Pharisees did not philosophise on the subject; but there is never any doubt as to the immense importance which they attached to *action*, as the most complete response which a man could make to any demand upon him. When, therefore, a man was confronted with the precepts in the Torah—" Thou shalt do " this and that, or " Thou shalt not do " so and so—both the doing of the thing commanded and the conscious intentional refusal of the thing forbidden were a definite committal of himself on the side of God, an express decision to make himself in that instance the instrument of the divine will.

Since, then, the conscious act possesses so great importance, it follows at once that the way in which the divine will should be done needs to be ascertaned with great care and very clearly defined. There must be, in every instance where God has given a command in the Torah, some one right way in which he desires that the required obedience shall be shown in act. That exactly right way must be contained in the Torah somewhere, either declared in so many words, or else to be inferred by competent interpretation. To make such inferences was the chief, if not the only, object of interpretation, as applied by the Pharisees to the preceptive part of the Torah. They set themselves to learn and to teach how a man should " walk in the ways of the Lord." And when they had defined such a rule of guidance, in respect of any one particular precept, they called that rule by the special name of 'Hălāchāh, which is derived from the Hebrew word meaning " to walk."

To define a Halachah was obviously to assume a very serious responsibility, because it really amounted to laying down the law for all who accepted the Pharisaic system. It was never allowed to any single teacher to fix the Halachah; that was only done after careful deliberation by the most experienced and respected teachers, and the decision was arrived at by the vote of the majority. Such decisions were carefully committed to memory and handed down, from teacher to disciple, for the guidance of future generations; for, while in one aspect they were only the decisions of a teaching body acting in council, in another aspect they were portions of the Torah made explicit which till then had not been known or understood.

The process here described was in operation before the New Testament period, indeed it must have begun when the Pharisees put forward their new theory of the Torah, as described above. It is this process which is referred to in the New Testament (Mark vii. 3) under the name of the Tradition of the Elders. The contents of that tradition, the things handed down, were so many defined Halachahs, rules of right conduct, each having the religious meaning and value already explained. In the time of Jesus the actual amount of defined Halachah was not great, at all events when compared with the immense number codified in the Mishnah at the beginning of the third century A.D. But the principle and the process of fixing the Halachah were already long established in his time; and Halachah, regarded as of vital importance for the reasons given above, was the special characteristic of the Pharisaic method in applying religion to life. We shall see later on that it was precisely the Halachah, the Tradition of the Elders, which formed the ground of opposition between Jesus and the Pharisees. It is also the ground for the charge of hypocrisy brought against them, in the New Testament and ever since. If a Pharisee was confronted by a precept of the Torah, he obeyed it in the way defined by the Halachah (supposing that in his time a Halachah had been defined upon that particular precept); and his obedience was expressed in an act of some kind. To a sincere Pharisee that act was a definite serving of God, an intentional doing of his will. The outward act alone was nothing without the inward intention. But the outward act was all that the onlooker could see; the inward intention was hidden from him, known only to God. It might accordingly happen, and did happen, that a professing Pharisee performed the outward act without the inward intention, and in that case his profession was a sham, and he a hypocrite. The Pharisees were very well aware of this danger, and they were quite as severe as Jesus himself was in their denunciation of hypocrites in their ranks. But also it might happen, and certainly did happen, that those who saw the outward act of the Pharisee and did not, because they could not, see the inward intention, wrongly judged him, and called him a hypocrite when he was, and knew that he was, perfectly sincere. A true Pharisee knew quite well that he could " tithe mint and anise and cummin and *not* leave undone the weightier matters of the Law, judgment, mercy and faith " (Matt. xxiii. 23). The Halachah of the Pharisees was an austere discipline, based on an intense desire to do the will of God, and by its peculiar form it exposed its adherents to the temptation of hypocrisy. Not all resisted that temptation, as is only to be expected, human nature being what it is ; but, when all is said and done, it was the Halachah which gave its strong support to the religion which has borne the name and inspired the noblest deeds of Judaism.

The Torah, as noted above, was the subject of interpretation by the Pharisees not only on its preceptive but also on its non-preceptive side. The object here was to draw forth all that could be learned from the revelation which God had given other than what was concerned with the doing of his will. The result of interpreting the Torah for this object was called *Hăggādāh*. What in other religions is dealt with under the heads of doctrinal and moral theology, Pharisaic and Rabbinic Judaism included under Haggadah. All teaching about the nature of God, his attributes, his government of the world, man and his relation to God and his fellow-men, all the subjects which furnish the problems of the philosophy of religion and of ethics, came within the scope of Haggadah. We shall see later on that there was a very considerable amount of common ground between the teaching of Jesus and that of the Pharisees. That common ground has reference to what was taught as Haggadah, though he himself did not teach it as such. He was not a Pharisee and did not use their methods, either that of Haggadah or that of Halachah; but he was a Jew and his teaching was for the most part markedly Jewish in form and substance, while arrived at from a direction other than that by which the Pharisees had come to their conceptions of religious truth.

Now while the Halachah was defined in clear rules of conduct, and moreover was binding upon all who accepted the Pharisaic discipline, the Haggadah was never developed into a system of theology and ethics and was not binding. One Halachah could not contradict another Halachah recognised as valid at one and the same time. An older Halachah might be modified, or replaced by a later one. But a Haggadah, setting forth some religious truth or ethical lesson, might express its meaning in one way and another Haggadah might express it in a different way, while yet both were received; indeed, the wide variety and frequent contradiction of Haggadah were taken to mean that God could teach many things through one text of the Torah, and that through such variety and even contradiction only so much the more was brought to light of the inexhaustible riches of the Torah as God's revelation.

Halachah and Haggadah together make up the Torah as interpreted, the whole of what at a given time has been made explicit, as compared with what still remains of undiscovered truth contained in the revelation. And when the Torah is called " the Law," the error is that only the Halachah is Law; the Haggadah is not Law, it is neither binding nor systematic, but is the result of allowing the imagination of devout minds to range freely over the subjects of religious thought and experience. Halachah and Haggadah are the creation of the Pharisees, and serve to distinguish them from all other types of Judaism. And both are the natural, and even necessary, result of their conception of the true significance of the Torah.

It is the purpose of this chapter to explain the formation of the different sects and parties to be found within Judaism in the New Testament period. Enough has perhaps been said in the foregoing pages to make it clear how there came to be the Sadducees and the Pharisees, and what they each stood for. It is well to bear in mind that both were included within the circle of Judaism, and that both shared in the inheritance of the religion as it had been held at the time of the return from the Exile. No doubt the Sadducees differed from the Pharisees in the way in which they regarded it; but of the general contents of the inherited religion as indicated above (pp. 16–19) no important item was affirmed by the one party and denied by the other.

It will be convenient to defer any further account of the teaching of the Pharisees, and of the Sadducees so far as it is known, until the account has been completed of the formation of sects and parties in Judaism. When that has been done, the reader will have before him a view of all the main types of

Judaism in the New Testament period, with some knowledge of how they came into existence and what phase of thought they represented. He will then realise what the Judaism was, in whose midst Christianity was born and spent its early years; and he will be in a position to understand both the points of close contact and those of sharp opposition between the old religion and the new, as expressed by the adherents of both. This will be dealt with in later chapters. For the present we resume the story of historical development.

The Sadducees and the Pharisees, when they emerge into the light of history, do so as two groups distinguished by name from each other and from the undefined mass of the Jewish people. This undefined mass came, indeed, to have a special name in the usage of the Pharisees, who referred to them as the People of the Land (Am hā-āretz). We shall have to study them closely if we are to understand the Judaism of the New Testament period; but for the present it will be better to direct our attention to the formation of the other sects and parties whose names were recited above (p. 40).

It will be remembered that the Maccabean revolt was due to the combination of two powerful motives in the minds of those who resisted Antiochus. These were, first, the desire to maintain the purity of the religion of Torah and freely to practise that religion, which was endangered by the assault of Hellenism; and, second, the desire for political freedom, national independence under a native ruler. Both these objects were attained; but there remained, in the minds of Jews under the Maccabean rule, the same two tendencies which had found expression in the revolt. There were those whose chief concern was the religion of Torah, and who stood aloof, so far as possible, from the politics of their time. There were also those who, while by no means indifferent to the religion of Torah as they understood it, combined with it a nationalist policy. When the breach between the Pharisees and the Sadducees took place, the former represented the purely religious tendency. They were never at any time a political party, although they were obliged, through the circumstances of the time, to make their influence felt in public affairs. They were strictly pacifist in their attitude towards the dissensions which rent the Maccabean kingdom and which led to the two great wars with Rome. They were never numerous; in the New Testament period there were only about six thousand Pharisees; but they had a powerful influence, through the Synagogues, over the mass of the people, and they exercised it on the side of religion, not of nationalism. The Sadducees, on the other hand, were so far in sympathy with the nationalist policy that they had no difficulty in supporting the political schemes of the Maccabean rulers, and may be said to belong to the governing class, if the term be permissible in a country which came to be ruled by Herod and finally fell a prey to Rome. But it is as doubtful whether the Sadducees ought to be called a political party, as it is difficult to see in them a purely religious sect. What is of chief importance is that the purely religious ideal and the nationalist ideal were both present to the Jewish mind from the time of the Maccabean revolt down to the final overthrow of the Jewish state in A.D. 135, and both these ideals, or rather the representatives of them, strove for the mastery. The various sects and parties, which came into being in the last century B.C. and endured throughout the New Testament period, owed their origin to one or another aspect of the conflict between these two ideals. And it must be carefully borne in mind that all of them, Essenes, Zealots, Apocalyptists and the rest (except the Herodians, of whom more will be said below), were Jews, and that the Torah was the common foundation of their religion. Whatever might divide them, they all took their stand on the Torah, but only the Pharisees held the peculiar conception of Torah described above. If an Apocalyptist or Apocryphal writer had much to say about the Torah, it is a complete mistake to assume that he was a Pharisee on that account. Whether he was or not depends on quite other considerations.

The history of the Jews during the century preceding the New Testament period is marked by increasing disorder, especially from the time, 63 B.C., when the Roman government began to take an active part in Jewish politics. The reigns of the last princes of the Maccabean family had been full of troubles, but at least that family was Jewish, and its founders had acquired a fame as national heroes which enabled even the last representatives of the family to find popular support in their struggles to recover their lost throne. But Herod, who sat on that throne, was no Jew; and his reign was an outrage both to the religious and nationalist feelings of his unwilling subjects. More cunning than Antiochus

Epiphanes, he took care to avoid a second Maccabean revolt; but, short of that, he was quite as intent on the Hellenising, or rather Romanising, of his kingdom. Ambitious, crafty, cruel and extravagant, Herod throughout his long reign (37–4 B.C.) wrought increasing misery to his subjects, through the oppression of heavy taxation, and exposed them to continual affront by his disregard of their religion and encouragement of everything Greek or Roman. This is Herod as he was seen and felt by the Jews; and, extremely able ruler though he was, it was not Jews who gave him his epithet of Great. The events of the century which closed with the death of Herod, and of the following century which saw the fall of Jerusalem, must be read of in the history books. The point of importance for the present purpose is that it was in this period of growing confusion, and especially during the reign of Herod, that the cause is to be found which led to the formation of the Essenes on the one hand and of the Zealots on the other, as sects or parties defined by name. The Essenes may have been an offshoot from the Pharisees; the Zealots were not Pharisees at all, any more than they were Sadducees. They represented a principle and a policy shared by neither of the two older parties.

As the growing oppression, in regard both to material welfare and to religious freedom, became to many Jews intolerable, it produced a reaction in each of two opposite directions. On the one hand, there were those who gave up the attempt to preserve their religion and fulfil its requirements amidst the trials and dangers to which they were exposed in the social life of cities and villages, and chose to withdraw into lonely places where they could form communities apart, where they could realise their ideal of the religious life in peace and safety. These were the Essenes, in whose case, also, the meaning of the name by which they were called is not certainly known. They were ascetics in their mode of life, and practised a degree of communism in their social organisation which suggests a monastery of later times. Like the monks, they withdrew from a wicked and cruel world, unable otherwise to maintain themselves in purity and holiness towards God. In strictness of life they were closely akin to the Pharisees; indeed their system might be called Pharisaism pushed to its logical extreme. But they differed from the Pharisees in two respects: first in their asceticism, and second in their isolation. Asceticism has never been generally approved, in Pharisaic and Rabbinic Judaism, as a right attitude towards life, while yet it is true that austere simplicity in regard to food and clothing was often practised and regarded with respect. But, in the view of the Pharisees, as of later Jews generally, all that the Creator had provided for the use of man was to be used, with thankfulness and with due moderation. God was not served if his gifts were refused, nor was it piety to neglect or ill-treat the body which he had made to be the companion of the soul. If it be allowable to speak of asceticism in connexion with Jews at all, even the Essenes, it was an asceticism which fell far short of the later Christian asceticism; for this on principle treated the body and its appetites as evil, and therefore to be subdued and coerced in every possible way. The Jewish ascetic never so far forgot the Creator in his treatment of the creature. And, in regard to the Essenes, there was probably no sharp line of division between them and the Pharisees in the matter of asceticism. There were certainly men who practised the austerest simplicity of life, as a way of holiness, who were closely akin to the Pharisees and who were to all appearance not Essenes. But the practice of living in secluded communities did mark the Essenes off from the Pharisees, both in practice and in principle. For the Pharisee held it to be the duty of every man to live in the world where God had placed him, to meet its temptations and trials, bear its burdens, face its dangers, and serve God in its midst, whatever the consequences might be. The reign of Herod, and the government of his successors down to the fall of Jerusalem, laid a burden of suffering upon all Jews, and tried their patience to the utmost. Yet the Pharisees bore it without flinching and without resisting, while the Essenes sought relief in flight and found peace by desertion. That as a rule the Essenes lived in isolated communities, mostly in the neighbourhood of the Dead Sea, is generally admitted; and the fact is not disproved by the occasional mention of an Essene living in ordinary intercourse with his fellow-men.

As the Essenes withdrew on principle from the common life of their countrymen, it is only natural that they should have left little if any mark upon that common life, whether in respect of religion or of anything else. Certainly the Judaism which survived, and which was the Judaism of the Pharisees, shows little or no trace of any Essene influence. The most that can be said is that possibly one or another of the chief Pharisaic teachers in the first century may have owed something to Essene self-discipline. Whether Christianity owes anything to the Essenes is a question which by many scholars is answered in the affirmative. Yet, considering that Jesus " came eating and drinking " and never set up or joined a community of recluses, there does not seem much to make it probable that he and his followers had any connexion with the Essenes. They are not mentioned either in the New Testament or in the Pharisaic literature. They are only known from the writings of Philo and Josephus; and it is allowable to suggest that their importance, either for Judaism or for Christianity, has been somewhat exaggerated. Insignificant in themselves, they serve to show one result of the oppression of the Jews in the time of Herod and after. They mark what may be called the negative reaction from that oppression.

At the opposite extreme from the Essenes were the Zealots, who represented the positive reaction. Their attitude towards oppression and the oppressor was not to retreat into safety, but to stand up and fight, to the death if need be. The Zealots are of immense importance in the Judaism of the New Testament period.

The name Zealot (Zēlōtēs) carries its meaning on its face, and is not shrouded in obscurity like " Pharisee," " Sadducee " and " Essene." It is the Greek rendering of the Hebrew *Kannai*, and

E

it simply means one who is zealous. The nearest equivalent in English would be "fanatic." For the Zealots, historically so called, were those among the Jews who were ready to go, and eventually did go, to the extreme limit of violence in the cause of the national religion and against the Gentile oppressor.

In their origin they were certainly a religious party, and for that reason they are properly included amongst the various representative types of Judaism at present under consideration. But that for which they became a party was not religion alone, or at least it was religion in its national aspect, the religion of the people whom JHVH had chosen, over whom he alone was the rightful king, so that his rights were infringed by all heathen cults, and it was his people who were oppressed and driven wild by heathen oppressors. There is no certain trace of the Zealots as a party until the end of the reign of Herod; but even at the beginning of his reign there were those whose actions were of a kind precisely like the deeds of the somewhat later Zealots. Hezekiah, whom Josephus called a robber-chieftain, was put to death by Herod at the beginning of his reign. His son was that Judas of Galilee who was the real founder of the Zealot party; but Hezekiah only did much what Judas did, and the so-called robber-chieftain, though he failed, sounded the first note of the rebellion, which became the great war of A.D. 66–70.

It is no doubt true that the Zealot party took definite shape as an organised body under Judas, about the year A.D. 6, when the census was taken by order of Quirinius; but their origin can be traced to an earlier date, with considerable probability. The Maccabean revolt had begun, in 167 B.C., by the sudden call of the priest Mattathias to resist the agents of the tyrant who would compel the Jews to disown their religion and disobey their God. Mattathias cried, "Whoso is *zealous* for the Torah . . . let him follow me" (1 Macc. ii. 27). The word translated "zealous" is (in Greek as well as in English) practically the same as the word "zealot." Moreover the Hebrew name *Kannaim*, which was the name of the party as organised by Judas of Galilee, is used in a law which dates from the Maccabean times. It would seem probable that Judas, when he organised the Zealots into a party, made it his object to repeat the exploits of the first Maccabeans, by violent measures against all who were disaffected in their adherence to the Torah and ready to submit to the heathen king. The rebellion begun by Judas Maccabæus had led to the liberation of the people from the foreign yoke and the establishment of an independent kingdom. That kingdom had only passed out of Maccabean hands when Herod acquired the throne; and the fact that every later attempt to recover it by his descendants found support amongst the people, shows that the memory of what the Maccabeans had done was still able to fire the popular mind in the time of Judas of Galilee. He, accordingly, like Mattathias, gathered around him those who were "zealous for the Torah," and they showed their zeal in much the same way. "And Mattathias and his friends went round about, and pulled down altars, and they circumcised by force the children that were uncircumcised, as many as they found within the borders of Israel. And they pursued after the sons of pride and the work prospered in their hands. And they rescued the Torah out of the hand of the Gentiles, and out of the hand of the kings, neither suffered they the sinner to triumph " (1 Macc. ii. 45–48).

Judas and his Zealots represented no new conception of Torah, as the Pharisees did ; rather they took it as it was, and laid stress on that side of it which needed no interpretation to make it plain. They proclaimed again that JHVH was the only King whom Jews ought to acknowledge, and that his kingdom could only be established by rooting out every trace of heathenism, breaking the yoke of tyranny from off the necks of the people. Whatever in the Torah enjoined the separation of Jew from Gentile, whatever exalted Israel as the Chosen People, and promised that they should triumph over the enemy and the oppressor, was made by the Zealots the chief content of their message ; and they enforced their arguments by the daggers which they carried with them, and which they so habitually used that " *Sicarii*," dagger-men, was one of the names by which they were known. It is not wonderful that a party so organised and pursuing such methods became in the end a mere horde of desperadoes, in whose wild excesses of ferocity all sense of order and high motive was lost. The movement which Judas of Galilee had definitely started passed beyond the control of those who tried to lead it, till its fury burned itself out in the last agony of Jerusalem. But, none the less, the original motive and inspiration of the Zealots was religious. For them, no less than for the Pharisees, the Sadducees and the Essenes, the Torah was the first and last word of religion. That was the common ground between them all. How the other three parties regarded the Torah has already been shown. The Zealots were not out to interpret the Torah, making it the subject of patient and peaceful study. They were out to fight for it, to assert all that was claimed in it for Israel and for the God of Israel, to suffer and die if need be in that one supreme cause.

This is what the Zealots certainly did; and it should not be necessary to point out that they could not be and were not Pharisees, as is often asserted. The Pharisees were, on principle, pacifists, and taught submission, not resistance, as being the will of God, in regard to his people, even under oppression. It was true that there was and could be only one rightful King over Israel, viz. God; but, until he saw fit to send his Messiah to establish his kingdom, no attempt ought to be made by human action to force his hand. The Pharisees, in fact, never coalesced with the Zealots, and it was against their will that they were swept into the raging torrent of the last war. By that time, of course, the Zealots had lost nearly all resemblance to what they had been at the outset; and it is quite likely, indeed it is certain, that at the outset, when Judas of Galilee organised his party, the Pharisees were not all of one mind about it. A Pharisee, by name Zadok, is said to have been associated with Judas in founding the party. And generally, those Pharisees who followed the lead of Shammai (who, along with Hillel, was one of the two chief teachers of the Pharisees at the time) were more inclined to sympathy with the Zealots than were the followers of Hillel. But however closely the Shammaite Pharisees approached to the Zealots, the fact remains that Pharisee and Zealot were two independent growths from the original Torah stock; and to identify them only leads to confusion and error.

More will be said in another connexion of the importance of a knowledge of the Zealots for the understanding of the Gospel story; but it may be useful to recall here that one of the twelve apostles was a Zealot, Simon Zelotes, whose other epithet Cananæan (Mark iii. 18) represents Kannai, or Zealot. It is probable that Judas Iscariot was also a Zealot. Also it is well to remember that the head-quarters of the Zealots were in Galilee, and that Judas the founder belonged to that country. It was he and his followers to whom Jesus referred when he said (Matt. xi. 12), " From the days of John the Baptist until now, the kingdom of heaven suffereth violence and men of violence take it by force."

Judas of Galilee is mentioned Acts v. 37, by Gamaliel, who was a Pharisee, and whose reference to Judas is certainly not in the tone of a sympathiser or admirer.

Of all the types of Judaism hitherto considered, the Zealots are the only ones with whom Jesus would have much opportunity of coming in contact. There were no Sadducees in Galilee; they had their head-quarters in Jerusalem as the seat of the Temple and the capital city. There were few Pharisees in Galilee, and none of the schools in which the Halachah was studied and defined. The Essenes lived in the desert by the Dead Sea, and had nothing to do with Galilee. Apart from the Zealots, Judaism was represented in Galilee by the undefined general population.

In the list given above (p. 40) of the several classes making up the population of Palestine, the next name after the Zealots is that of the *Herodians*. They are mentioned in the Gospels (Matt. xxii. 16, Mark xii. 13) and are possibly referred to in the saying of Jesus (Mark viii. 15) to his disciples, bidding them " beware of the leaven of the Pharisees and of the leaven of Herod." But beyond the obvious fact of some connexion with Herod there is no evidence to show who the Herodians were, or what they stood for. In the absence of all data on which to base an opinion, it has even been found possible to maintain that the Herodians believed Herod the Great to be, or to have been, the Messiah. They are mentioned here merely for the sake of completeness. It is not certain that they were a religious party, and it is possible that they were not Jews.

We have now surveyed the various sects and parties amongst the Jews which were distinguished from each other by special names, and have learned to understand how they severally came into being, and what general principle each represented. But these named classes by no means cover the whole of the Jewish people, considered with reference to their religion. Indeed, it is probable that all four classes together do not make up more than a small fraction of the whole Jewish population. We have therefore to study now the unnamed mass of the Jewish population, from the point of view of its religion.

To call it "unnamed" is not strictly correct, because the Pharisees, at all events, had a general name for them and referred to them as the "People of the Land," in Hebrew Am hā-āretz. The name should be remembered, as it is of importance for the understanding of the relation of Jesus to the Judaism of his time and country; but it should be borne in mind that Am ha-aretz is not the name of a sect or party representing some one principle of belief or action. It is a name under which the Pharisees included all Jews who did not come up to the Pharisaic standard of precise observance. Presumably they would regard Sadducees as Am ha-aretz, and possibly Essenes and Zealots also; but there is no need to raise the point, and Am ha-aretz may be taken to mean all Jews not otherwise specified by a distinctive name indicating their religious position.

It is clear that the Am ha-aretz were not all of one type, either in respect of their religion or socially and economically. Just as they included rich and poor, capitalist and labourer, the merchant, the farmer, the artisan, the tax-gatherer (publican) and the tradesman, so, on the religious side, they included those who were just not Pharisees, and those who paid little or no heed to religion at all, with every shade of piety or indifference in between. Nothing that is said about the Am ha-aretz, in the Talmud or elsewhere, can be taken to refer to all who were included under that name; and, conversely, statements which may be made about them are not proved to be incorrect by the fact that instances may be given where those statements do not apply. Thus, there were Synagogues of the Am ha-aretz ; and though the Pharisees, or some of them, might disapprove of such places as being less strict than they ought to be, yet people who cared nothing for religion would certainly not take the trouble to go there. Many people, in Christian countries, go to a place of worship, and like to go there, who do not in all respects come up to its standard of belief or practice. No one was obliged to go to Synagogue, and some people went there only seldom or not at all, while yet they were all Am ha-aretz. Some of them reviled the Pharisaic teachers, who spoke of them in very severe terms ; but here also the statement only applies to some, perhaps only a very few, certainly not to all of the Am ha-aretz. It would be certain, without the express testimony of Josephus, that the Pharisees had very great influence over the general mass of the Jewish population, *i.e.* the Am ha-aretz, and were held by them in great respect as religious teachers ; which shows that the Am ha-aretz were by no means wholly estranged from religion, though some were.

It was chiefly, perhaps wholly, through the Synagogues that the Pharisees made their influence felt. The Synagogues, as shown above, were entirely under the guidance of the Pharisees, without whom there would probably have been no Synagogues, at all events as late as the New Testament period. How far the influence of the Pharisees was felt outside the Synagogues it would be hard to say. It does not appear that they made any direct efforts, as religious teachers, to get hold of the outsiders, who never went to Synagogue; though the example of Christian countries shows how the influence of a place of worship in a village or town is felt by many who never go there, through the character of the regular attendants and of their leader. Those of the Am ha-aretz who, for one reason or another, never went to Synagogue, were to that extent outside the influence of the Pharisees; and such, whether few or many, were those whom Jesus saw " as sheep without a shepherd " (Mark vi. 34). The fact that he went to them and talked to them wherever he found them, in the fields or by the lake, on the hillside or in the village street, was something new in their experience. And Jesus was an Am ha-aretz himself.

Before concluding this chapter, we must complete the list given above by mentioning the Proselytes. These were persons who adopted the Jewish religion, having previously held some form of heathen religion. Obviously they were not a sect or party, like those already studied. They simply accepted the Jewish religion, and they might, in theory at least, attach themselves to any one of the sects or parties already described. In practice, however, their religion as Jews was probably most nearly allied to the Pharisaic type, since it was the Synagogue which gave to the interested inquirer the best opportunity of knowing what Judaism was as a religion. Some Gentiles went the whole length of conversion to Judaism by submitting to the rite of circumcision and accepting the duty of fulfilling all the requirements of the Halachah. These were known as " proselytes of righteousness," and these are the only real proselytes recognised in Judaism. But there were other people who, without going so far, worshipped the one God, observed the Sabbath and in general adopted the Jewish religion as an ethical monotheism, while not complying with all its ritual requirements. These were not proselytes and were never called so. Yet they were obviously different from the ordinary Gentile. They were called " Fearers of God," and formed a sort of fringe to the strictly Jewish community. They were to be found attending in the Synagogues, and are mentioned in the New Testament as such (Acts xiii. 16, and elsewhere). The term " proselyte of the gate," sometimes supposed to denote a sort of half convert, is not found in Jewish sources till as late as the thirteenth century, and then only as a paraphrase of " The stranger who is in thy gates " (Exod. xx. 10, and elsewhere). The only two classes recognised in Judaism, other than the Jew by birth and bringing up, were the convert who accepted the whole of Judaism, and the resident alien who was not a Jew at all, not even a convert, though he might be one of " those that fear God."

The Pharisees were charged by Jesus (Matt. xxiii. 15) with " compassing sea and land to make one proselyte." Considering that in their view to convert a Gentile was to bring him to the knowledge and service of the one God, it was only natural and right that they should make such efforts ; and it is certain that in a quiet way a good deal of missionary work was done, chiefly through the Synagogues. The two great wars, and the final overthrow of the Jewish national life, put an end to such missionary work. Opinions varied amongst the leading Pharisaic teachers upon the question whether proselytes were to be encouraged or not, and whether they were a good or an evil for Judaism. But the question is not of importance in regard to the Judaism with which the New Testament is concerned.

We have now made a general survey of the Jewish people, in the period with which we are concerned, so far as regards their religion. When a whole population is concerned, it goes without saying that it must include good, bad and indifferent—people who take their religion seriously and people who think little or nothing about it. Moreover, in regard to the sects and parties distinguished by specific names, these indicate groups of persons in whose minds some main principle was, so to speak, brought to a focus and made prominent, rather than groups marked off from each other by rigid lines of exclusion. It is true that the Pharisees were definitely grouped in societies and formed a sort of closed corporation, to which no one was admitted except on compliance with stringent conditions. But it is none the less true that the Pharisees had an influence far beyond the limits of their defined society, because what they really stood for, as already explained, was the application of the religion of Torah, as a living religion, to the whole of life. Beyond any question, Pharisaism was the element in Judaism wherein lay most of its vitality, as is shown by the fact that Pharisaism was the only type of Judaism which survived the wreck of the Jewish state. Its influence radiated as from a centre through the whole of the Jewish population, chiefly through the Synagogues ; so that the mass of the people, while not being themselves Pharisees, revered them as those always are revered who really set themselves to live their religion.

Neither the Sadducees nor the Essenes wielded an influence over the people which could for a moment be compared with that of the Pharisees. The Essenes could not do so, being out of sight and out of mind to the population as a whole. The Sadducees do not appear to have taken any account of the people at large, being concerned with the Temple, as the sufficient symbol and expression of the national religion, and with their own position as ministers thereof and interested in its maintenance.

But with the Zealots the case was very different. They could make an appeal to the people other than that of the Pharisees, and were able at times to overcome it with their clamour and silence it by their violence. Like all Jews, the Zealots took their stand on the Torah, and for that reason they could offer a challenge which no Jew could wholly disregard. They appealed to all who were " zealous for the Torah " to join them in fighting for it. The Pharisees were as zealous for the Torah as the Zealots were, but they repudiated violence as the true way of showing their zeal and of obeying God who had given the Torah. They had only a quiet lesson of submission to teach, of trust in God and of waiting his time. The Zealots came with the burning words of men smarting under cruelty at the hands of heathen oppressors—Herod or the Romans, it was all one. The God of Israel mocked at and defied, his holy Torah set at nought, his chosen people made the victims of their enemies—was it not the duty of every Jew to rise up and fight, even to the death if need be, against such intolerable wrong ? Why wait for God to send the Messiah to establish his kingdom ? Why not bring it at once, and usher in the final triumph of Israel over the " wicked kingdom " ? No wonder that the influence of the Zealots made itself powerfully felt, especially when supported by murders and assassinations and the lawless violence of would-be rebels. It was an influence working across that of the Pharisees, and at times overmastering it ; but it was fundamentally opposed to theirs and they felt it, while yet they were quite as much aware of the cruelty and oppression as the Zealots were. A Pharisee might sincerely disapprove of the Zealot policy and of the ideas which underlay it, while smarting under the wrongs which prompted it and sharing the indignation which those wrongs called forth.

So, in the period with which we are concerned, Judaism was the religion of the Jewish people, showing itself in such different types as have been described, with the Torah for its base, and chiefly the two powerful influences of the Pharisees and the Zealots as the moving forces which determined its action. The Pharisees, strictly defined, were only a small group ; and the Zealots, the actual band who followed Judas, may have been as small in number. The Am ha-aretz, the general Jewish population, were drawn this way and that; now following the lead of the Pharisees and remaining quiet, carrying on their daily work as well as they could in such troubled times, and then in despair throwing in their lot with the Zealots, crowding into the army which defended Jerusalem in A.D. 70 against the Roman army, and that which made the last stand fighting around Bar Cocheba in Bether in 135.

CHAPTER III

THE TEACHING OF THE PHARISEES

It has been shown, in the previous chapter, that the Jewish people in the New Testament period included certain groups, bearing specific names and representing different religious views. The Am ha-aretz, the Jewish population generally, was by no means without religion; but it would not be true to say that it had a definite type of religion which marked it off from that of the Pharisees or the Sadducees, the Essenes or the Zealots, as possessing something which these others had not got. The popular religion was fostered by the Synagogue, and thus was in all essentials Pharisaic, so far as it went. How far it went, towards strict observance and severe piety in the one direction or laxity and indifference in the other, varied with each individual case.

To present the Judaism of the New Testament period as that which was believed and practised by all or by most Jews at that time, it will be necessary to describe those of the different groups, so far as they are known, bearing in mind that all represented varying types of one fundamental religion. Pharisees and Sadducees were sharply divided from each other, both on the vitally important question of the validity of the oral tradition, as already explained, and upon other specific points of doctrine. But both alike were Jews, and as such occupied a very large extent of common ground. And the same is true of the other groups. In the New Testament period Judaism for all Jews was based on the Torah, and it included the contents of the older religion which had survived the Exile and been handed down alike by the priests and the scribes.

Of all the groups representing Judaism, already named, the Pharisees are the only ones whose religious views are known with any approach to completeness. In regard to the others, some points of difference are singled out for special mention, while agreement on others is assumed as probable rather than known for certain. The Pharisees have left a literature of enormous extent, in which Pharisaism, in its length and breadth and height and depth, is faithfully portrayed. The Sadducees have left little or nothing of the same kind. The Essenes are known to have had sacred books, but it is not known what those books contained. Of Zealot literature, indeed, there are considerable remains, in the Apocryphal and especially the Apocalyptic books, usually ascribed to the Pharisees but with which the Pharisees had nothing to do.

It will best serve the purpose in hand to describe first of all the main contents of the religion of the Pharisees, and afterwards to add such features as are characteristic of the other groups. The reason for taking this course is not merely the fact, stated above, that the literary presentation of Pharisaism is far more complete than that of the other groups, but that in the period with which we are concerned

F

the influence of Pharisaism as a factor in Judaism was more powerful and more widely felt than that of any of the other groups. It is true that the influence of the Zealots was at times even more powerful than that of the Pharisees, and violently deflected the mind of the Jewish people from its normal course. But the Zealot influence was temporary, while that of the Pharisees was permanent and was thus able to reassert itself after the perturbing force of the Zealots had ceased to act.

The account which will be given below of the main contents of Pharisaism as a body of teaching is based upon the Rabbinic literature, which is the only recognised and legitimate authority for any statement upon the subject. And this position is deliberately taken and maintained, in face of the plausible objection, very often made, that the Rabbinic literature is almost entirely of later date than the New Testament period, and therefore cannot be used as a witness of what was current belief in that period, more particularly in the time of Jesus. Fully to discuss this objection would be impossible without an amount of reference to passages in the Talmud and Midrash quite outside the scope of this book. But enough can, it is hoped, be said to show why it is legitimate to use the Rabbinic literature for the purpose of illustrating the Judaism of the New Testament period in general and that of the time of Jesus in particular. And one incidental result of doing so will be to throw a good deal of rather unexpected light upon the question why so much of the teaching ascribed to Jesus is palpably Jewish in form.

The reader is reminded of the distinction drawn in the preceding chapter (above, pp. 54–57) between Halachah and Haggadah.   With the former we are not at present concerned.   But Haggadah was described as interpretation of Torah on its non-preceptive side, the purpose being not to define rules of right conduct, but to draw forth lessons of religion, to set forth truth in regard to all that concerns God and man in themselves and in their relation to each other—all, in short, that in other fields of religious thought is included in doctrinal theology and ethics.   Now the contents of Judaism, as a body of religious beliefs and ethical teaching, are to be found in the Haggadah.   The Halachah is a specialised application of the fundamental Jewish belief about God and man's duty towards him ; but the belief itself can be stated without reference to the Halachah, however necessary be the inference of the one from the other.

The Haggadah, then, is the chief source of information as to what was believed and taught in regard to the theology and ethics of Judaism, and Haggadah is found in large amount scattered up and down in the Talmud, and collected into separate commentaries known as Midrashim.   These were all edited in their present form at dates of which the earliest is considerably later than the New Testament period.   But they are all traditional, and the tradition, in the form of utterances by named teachers, goes back to a time well within the New Testament period, though very seldom as early as the time of Jesus.   Now it is a fact, well known to all students of the Rabbinic literature, that the main beliefs which find expression in the Haggadah are much the same, in the earliest as in the latest Midrashim, however varied the illustration of them given by this or that teacher. The Haggadah was never worked up into a system of theology, nor developed along lines of definite advance from an earlier to a later stage. Such advance can be traced in Christian theology, because that was systematic and its object was to define the true faith, to state with precision what the Church held, and required its adherents to hold, to be the truth. There is in Christian theology a right place for a history of doctrine; there is none in Jewish theology, or only to a very slight extent, so far as can be judged from the voluminous Haggadah that has come down to us.

If, therefore, the main contents of Jewish theology are on the whole the same at the earliest point to which they can be traced back as they are in succeeding centuries, the question arises, Are we entitled to draw the conclusion that they were also the same, on the whole, at a still earlier period, say the time of Jesus or even before his time? This conclusion would be unwarranted if it could be shown that any break had occurred, leaving its traces in the earliest Haggadah known to us, or if teaching now found in the Haggadah had been met by a challenge from some Scribe or Pharisee as being new and unheard of. But there is no sign of any breach of continuity made previous to the earliest known Haggadah, and leaving traces to show that a new departure had been made. And while it is perfectly true that some of the teaching of Jesus was challenged by the Pharisees, as being an innovation of which they strongly disapproved, it is also true that against a great deal of his teaching they made no protest whatever, accepting it without question or remark, as being what they themselves were accustomed to teach. This being so, then the conclusion is justified that what is found in the extant Haggadah is on the whole much the same as what was believed and taught at least as early as the time of Jesus, and probably earlier still; and that it is legitimate to use the literature, which is in form later but in substance only slightly affected by the lapse of time, to illustrate the contents of Judaism in the New Testament period.

The Christian reader, if he is to understand Judaism on its theological side, must put out of his mind (and keep out of it) the idea that definite doctrines were formulated and taught upon the several topics of theology. The teaching in the Synagogue, which was entirely on Pharisaic lines, was given by men whose sole object was to develop and strengthen in their hearers religion as they knew it in their own experience and held it in their own belief. Thus, they had a strong and deep belief in God as the Father in Heaven, the Sovereign Lord, the Creator, the Ruler, the Judge; but they did not define a doctrine setting forth the truth and guarding against possible error in regard to God. Accurate definition, on this and similar subjects, lay outside the range of their thought. What they did was to speak of God as they believed him to be, and in their experience felt him to be, and to speak of him thus to men who in some degree shared their belief and experience. If they were to speak of him at all, they must put their thoughts and beliefs into words, with what clearness and force they could. But from first to last they were religious teachers, and neither theologians nor philosophers. And so of every other subject which formed part of the contents of their religion. A survey of those contents will, accordingly, give a summary of what was generally believed and taught in the Synagogues, there being no requirement of anything like doctrinal uniformity, nor any guarantee that every individual Jew did as a matter of fact hold every belief included in that summary.

A further remark is necessary. The Jew, and especially the Pharisee, attached very great importance to the doing of God's will, and he found in the Halachah (see above, p. 54) the guidance he needed, so far as Halachah had been defined in his time. To obey the divine will, as exactly as he knew how, was the highest of all duties; but that is not to say that the doing of acts so prescribed was the whole of his religion. In a sense, it was not even his religion at all, but a necessary consequence of his religion. The Halachah was a definition of some of the contents of the Torah; the Torah was what God had revealed. The Halachah would have been meaningless, and the Torah a delusion, unless behind both was God—owned, feared, loved, trusted, worshipped, in the inward life of the soul. And the passionate devotion which is so abundantly expressed in the Pharisaic literature, for the Torah and for the Halachah as a special interpretation of it, is really a devotion felt towards God, expressing itself in terms of what was owned to be his most signal blessing. Therefore, when Pharisaic Judaism is represented, as it usually is, as a barren and unspiritual formalism, the description is entirely untrue, because the whole of what gave meaning and living power to the Pharisaic conception of religion is left out and ignored, even its existence being seldom suspected. The summary to be given, of the main contents of the religion of the Pharisees, will indicate what was in the minds of those who could and did spend infinite pains in defining niceties of conduct upon points which in themselves were of no importance.

In regard to the belief in God, there was no breach between the Pharisees and the prophets of the earlier time, who had raised to its highest point the conception of God as the one and only divine being, maker of heaven and earth. And while it is true that the Pharisees were (like all other Jews) the inheritors of the older Scriptures, in which other and less exalted conceptions of God were represented, yet the chief stress in the later Judaism was laid upon the loftier conceptions of the divine nature. The prophets had left little or nothing more to be said in regard to the sovereignty of God, the one only True, before whom " all the gods of the nations are idols." The Pharisees believed what Isaiah had said, in words which were spoken once for all. But they developed the belief in God beyond the point at which the prophets had left it, and in perhaps the only direction in which development was possible. They laid stress upon the nearness of God and the personal relation to him of the individual soul. This was a natural consequence of that individualising of religion which, as was shown above (p. 21), was one main feature distinguishing the Judaism of the period after the Exile from the religion of Israel before that time. It is often said that the tendency in the later Judaism, in the centuries after the Exile and down to the time of Jesus, was to remove God, in thought, further and further away, so that he became more and more of an abstraction and less and less of a felt and known reality. So far is this statement from being true that it was just in those centuries that the conception of God in Judaism was taken furthest away from lofty abstraction and brought nearest to human apprehension in a close personal relationship. Isaiah had said, "Thus saith the High and Lofty one who inhabiteth eternity, whose name is holy, I dwell in the high and holy place, with him also that is of a contrite and humble spirit, to revive the spirit of the humble and to revive the heart of the contrite one" (Isa. lvii. 15). The Pharisees took up the second half of that great saying, while they left the first as it was. They had nothing to add to the thought of the sublimity of God, but they found a great deal to say about his nearness, his care for his creatures, his love for his children. And it was in the period between the Exile and the time of Jesus that the term "Father in Heaven" was first used in addressing God or speaking of him. That great phrase came into use amongst the Pharisees, certainly before, probably long before, the time of Jesus. It does not occur in the Old Testament, but is clearly foreshadowed there. And it was in every way natural that those who inherited, not merely the letter but also the spirit of the older Scriptures, should have made their way to the thought of the close personal relation between God and the soul which found expression in the marvellous simplicity of the term Father in Heaven. Once the thought had been clothed in the fitting words, the term took its place in the customary language of the Synagogue, where, in course of time, Jesus naturally learned to use it. Through him it passed into Christian use, where it has remained ever since; but it was first uttered by Jewish lips, and what it means was first realised in Jewish minds, pondering " the deep things of God." If the tendency of Judaism in the centuries after the Exile had been to remove God in thought from human apprehension, it is inconceivable that the term Father in Heaven should have been devised or deemed appropriate, since, in that case, the spiritual need which it was intended to satisfy would not have been felt.

The question will be asked whether the term Father in Heaven in Jewish usage meant that God was the Father of all men or of Jews only? It would certainly be untrue to say that the acknowledged Jewish teachers in any age, before or after the rise of Christianity, have limited the conception of the Fatherhood of God to his special relation with the Jews. Judaism, in one of its aspects, was, and is, a universal religion, while in another aspect it was, and is, a national religion. How the two aspects are to be recognised and harmonised is one of the problems of Judaism. But neither was ever held to the entire exclusion of the other, while it is true, as indeed is only natural, that the national or particular aspect was more often and more clearly present to the Jewish consciousness than the universal aspect. The mass of mankind were without that knowledge of God which had been revealed to Israel in the Torah; and thus, while God was the Father in Heaven in regard to all men, only the Jews knew him as such. When therefore, in the prayers of the Synagogue, Jews prayed to him as " Our Father who art in Heaven," it is only likely that they were most conscious of what he was to them, in their own experience; but, if they had been challenged to say whether he was also the Father of men in general, the answer " that he was not " would be seldom heard, and never with general acceptance.

The term Father in Heaven was not the only, nor even the most usual, mode of referring to God or of addressing him. The ancient name JHVH (believed to have been pronounced Jahveh) was no longer used, except by the High Priest at certain special moments in the Temple service. Probably the most usual designation of God was " The Holy One, blessed be He." Other terms were " Lord of the Worlds," " The Place " (meaning the All-present), " The King of the kings of the kings." The actual word meaning God (El or Elohim) was very seldom used, and the modes of address just mentioned were intended to avoid the necessity of directly naming God. With the same intention the word " Heaven " was substituted for " God " in such phrases as " The Kingdom of Heaven " (= of

God); and the direct agency of God and his invisible presence were indicated by the terms Memra (word or act) and Shechinah (dwelling). But there was never any intention in the mind of the Pharisees (or probably of any other Jews) of regarding these as divine beings subordinate to the one supreme God. Judaism has never let go the idea of the divine Unity, nor admitted any kind of qualification of that Unity, as by the recognition of a mediator or some supposed second God. And, whatever was said and believed about God, as indicated in the names mentioned above, nothing was allowed to interfere with the belief in his nearness, his individual care for human souls. The belief in the existence of angels, and of good and evil spirits—a belief which was probably held by all Jews in the New Testament period, with the exception of the Sadducees—had no effect in removing God to a distance from direct human apprehension; nor was it the result of a belief in his remoteness, for there was no such belief. It was simply a picturesque way of filling out the idea of God as King, an Eastern king being attended by a vast train of courtiers and servants. Angels and spirits, including what are called " devils " in the New Testament, belonged to folklore and popular superstition or fancy, they had no place in religion. A Jew might believe in angels, but he never prayed to an angel; and, however much he might regard himself as under the influence of good or evil spirits, it was always God whose blessing he owned or whose protection he sought.

The belief in God described above was not

systematised in a theology nor based upon a philosophy. Attempts in these directions were not made till long after the New Testament period. The Jew of that period believed that God was the Lord of all worlds, the one Holy, Wise, Just and Good, the Sovereign Ruler of all mankind. He also believed that God was near " in every kind of nearness " to his children on earth. How these two aspects of God were to be combined and harmonised was a question which never troubled his devout belief, still less pressed for an answer. He prayed to God as " Our Father and our King," and does so to the present day, because both terms have a meaning in which he can find satisfaction for real spiritual needs.

The further presentation of the belief in God will best be made after a survey of the Pharisaic ideas concerning the nature of man. For this will make possible the study of the relation between God and man, upon which so much depends that is characteristic of Judaism. Here also, as in the case of the belief in God, the Pharisees inherited the teaching of the older Scriptures in regard to the nature of man, and, except in one direction, made no important advance upon that teaching. They regarded man as a being different from all others in possessing (or consisting of) both body and soul. He was a creature, like everything else in the world, but he was made in the image and likeness of God. However close might be the relation between them, man was distinct from God, and no blending of the two was ever thought of. Man was the creature, the subject, and the child of

God; but the line of demarcation between them, wherever it might be drawn, remained ineffaceable.

Man was a free moral agent, whose obedience to the divine will it was in his own power to give or to withhold. This is expressly stated in the Pharisaic literature; but it is implied in the attitude of mind which regards God as the righteous Judge and the Father in Heaven.

The twofold nature of man, as consisting of soul and body, was taken to mean that the soul inhabited the body but that both were from God, the soul being that which was made in the divine image and likeness, and the body being its temporary abode, assigned by God and committed to the care of its indweller during the time they were associated. The body was to be treated with proper respect, and the natural functions of the body were to be looked on as what God had ordained. They were not to be suppressed, but controlled. Asceticism, in the sense of exalting the spirit by crushing and defying the body, was never countenanced by the Pharisees, though it may have been to some extent by the Essenes. But rigorous simplicity of living, which is not the same as asceticism, was included, though not required, in the Pharisaic conception of the highest type of life, and examples of it are found in their literature. On this side there was probably no sharp line of division between Pharisees and Essenes; and it is on this ground that John the Baptist is by some thought to have been an Essene, as he certainly was not a Pharisee. The general line taken by the Pharisees (followed by all later Jews) was that every gift of the Creator should be regarded as good and used with moderation, in subjection to the claims of higher duties.

The most important advance made by the Pharisees beyond the Old Testament teaching as to the nature of man, was the doctrine (if the term be allowed) of the two Impulses (*yetzer*). Every man is created with two tendencies or impulses, of which the one inclines him to good and the other to evil. Both of these impulses, and not alone the good one, are implanted in human nature by the Creator. The evil impulse is the occasion of temptation to sin, or more exactly it is that which makes the occasion into a means of temptation. Man is free to choose whether he will yield to the good impulse or the bad; and the only constraint upon his power to act according to his choice is that which he has made for himself by the cumulative force of habit. He can become the slave of the evil impulse, but the possibility always remains for him to free himself from the bondage, by the help of God. When it is said, in the Lord's Prayer, "Deliver us from evil," or, as in the Revised Version, "from the evil *one*," the reference is probably to the evil impulse just described. Belief in devils, and in a prince of the devils, was no doubt common, but it was not usual to refer to the latter as the Evil One, or to ascribe to him the agency in temptation to sin. The Epistle of James expresses the Jewish view when it says (Jas. i. 14), "Every man is tempted when he is drawn away by his own lust and enticed." The phrase "his own lust" corresponds to the evil impulse, and is not restricted to the specific meaning of sexual desire, though that is included.   Paul was well aware of the Jewish doctrine of the two impulses, as can be seen in the Epistle to the Romans, especially chapter vii; but, when he says that the spirit and the flesh are opposed to each other (Gal. v. 17), it must be observed that Jewish thought never identified " the flesh " with the evil impulse, nor regarded flesh and spirit as hostile to one another.   This would be one of the points of opposition between Paul and his Jewish antagonists.   His entire doctrine of sin is quite un-Jewish.

Having now surveyed the beliefs of the Pharisees in regard to God and in regard to man, we go on to consider their ideas as to the relation in which they stood to each other.   This is indicated by the names used in reference to God, as enumerated above, and is expressed in the terms Creator and creature, Ruler and subject, Father and child.   On the divine side, towards the human, there is blessing —help, guidance, protection, care, providential bounty, mercy, forgiveness, love—as the case may be.   On the human side, towards the divine, there is obedience, trust, aspiration, penitence, humility, and again love.   There is communion between them, from God to man in the form of revelation, from man to God in the form of prayer.

This is, in theory, the relation between God and every human being; but it is nowhere found completely realised.   Revelation is, in fact, given to Israel alone; the rest of mankind are in ignorance, and can only come to the knowledge of the divine truth through the agency of Israel.   And prayer, for want of the knowledge of God, is almost meaningless outside the community of Israel. Further, the relation between God and man, which ought to be one of harmony between the human will and the divine, is interrupted (though not destroyed) by sin, which is wilful disobedience. It can only be restored by repentance on the human side and forgiveness on the divine side.

This very compressed summary needs to be expanded in fuller detail. And first, of the exceptional position held by Israel in the general relation between God and man. It has been shown above that Judaism was, and is, in one aspect a universal religion, and in another aspect a national religion. God was worshipped as the One only God, Maker of Heaven and Earth; but he was also regarded as the God of Israel. The great prophet who laid most stress upon the one aspect of God is the most emphatic in maintaining the other (Isa. xliii. 10–15). This twofold aspect of God passed unchanged into the religion of the Jews after the Exile, and has remained a vital element in Judaism ever since. The Pharisees were quite aware of the contradiction between the universal and the particular in their thought of God, and in the character of their religion in consequence. They did not discuss it as a theological or philosophical problem; they firmly believed in both aspects, as equally guaranteed by revelation; and, as regarded the second, the national aspect, confirmed by the history of the nation from the beginning. The divine revelation was contained in the Torah, given to Moses and to all Israel through him. As a matter of fact, no other nation was in possession of the Torah; and this was accounted for (probably later than the New Testament period) by saying that the Torah was offered to all the nations, in the most public manner possible, but refused by all except Israel. The Torah was the revelation of the will of God, and of such truth as he chose to impart. The giving and accepting of the Torah constituted the relation between God and Israel as that of a covenant between them, in which blessing was promised on the one side and obedience pledged on the other. Israel did thus stand in a relation towards God unlike that of any other nation; and this was expressed in the belief that God had chosen Israel out of all the rest of mankind, a belief which is clearly stated in the older Scriptures. But the divine choice laid on Israel a burden of responsibility—the duty of being witnesses for God to mankind and of making known the truth concerning him, proclaiming the religion which had the One only God for the object of worship. If it was an honour and a privilege to have been so chosen, it was full of danger and exposed the bearer of it to the ill-will and jealousy of his fellow-men. In this way the difficulty was got over of combining a religion meant for all mankind, and to which they were invited, with a religion confined in actual fact to one single nation. Israel was to be the missionary of the One God to the human race, and the particular characteristics of Judaism in its national aspect were intended to mark him out and qualify him for his task. It was in accordance with this view that efforts were made to convert Gentiles to Judaism, and to admit them as proselytes (see above, p. 74). But there

G

was never any such missionary enterprise on a large scale as is found in Christianity.

To return now to the study of the relation between God and man. Revelation was the act of the former towards the latter, and what was revealed was all comprised in the Torah, and for practical purposes was confined to Israel. From the human side to the divine, the relation between them implied the offering of prayer as a real communion. Prayer was one of the vitally important elements in the religion of the Pharisees, on precisely the same grounds as those on which it is a vitally important element in the Christian religion. They were well aware of the danger of formalism, and careful to guard against it; but prayer remained for them the central act of the spiritual life, the soul's utterance to the listening God. It was never characteristic of the Pharisees to pray after the manner described in Luke xviii, 11, 12.

In Revelation and Prayer the relation between God and man becomes actual, as a reality of experience. In revelation is given that which man needs to know for his spiritual welfare; and through prayer he draws from the divine source of all blessing the help and strength that he needs, or pours out his gratitude or his penitence. This is true in all spiritual religions, and it is true in Pharisaism. Peculiar to the Pharisees was the form in which they expressed their belief as to the contents of revelation, and the consequent effect upon man of the reception of those contents. We have seen that the Torah, which contained the whole of revelation, as the Pharisees understood it, was interpreted along two lines, according as the subject-matter was of the nature of precept or otherwise. The result in the one case was termed Halachah, in the other Haggadah. The purpose for which the Torah was given and the Halachah defined was that man should do the will of God, and do it in exactly the right way. If therefore the relation between God and man were completely realised there would be perfect obedience, perfect harmony between the human will and the divine. There would be thankfulness for the opportunity given to serve God, and there would be joy in the consciousness of having done so. Every command, whether written in Scripture, or defined in a Halachah, or owned in conscience, or prompted by the natural feeling of the heart, was such an opportunity of serving God. It was an occasion on which to fulfil the precept, " Thou shalt love the Lord thy God." The more such occasions were multiplied, the more completely a man could make his life a service of God. Such an occasion, arising out of a precept, was called a mitzvah, which means " command "; and, on Pharisaic lines, it was the sheer goodness of God which provided them so abundantly. To do a mitzvah was the highest that a man could do; but only if he did it as intending to serve God thereby. Merely to do the prescribed act without the intention was worthless, and to do so deliberately was hypocrisy.

From this conception of " the whole duty of man " the Pharisees drew two conclusions, which they expressed in terms of two familiar words—Reward and Merit. They believed, and taught quite explicitly, that there was a reward for fulfilling a precept, and that a man acquired merit by doing so. If Christians who have expressed strong disapproval of this teaching had grasped the meaning of it they would have been less ready to condemn it, and they would better have understood what Jesus meant when he used the same terms.

The idea of Reward was derived from the older Scriptures where it is quite plainly indicated, usually in terms of material prosperity. The Pharisees never rejected this view, but they developed the idea of reward far beyond the point at which it was left in Scripture, and they tended more and more to dwell on the spiritual as distinguished from the material aspect of it. In brief their line of thought was this :—To do the will of God is the highest duty of man. God is just ; and therefore he cannot be indifferent as to whether a man does his will or does not do it. In some way it must be, and actually is, better for the man who does his will than for the man who does not do it. In the sight of God there is a difference between saint and sinner ; and in the experience of each there is also a difference. The *better condition* in which the man is who does the will of God, is what the Pharisees meant by reward. It was not of the nature of a bribe, or an offer of payment, part of a bargain made for the purpose of securing blessings from God. It was the consequence which followed when a man did his best to serve God. And what the Pharisees meant by it could not be better expressed than in the words : " Well done, good and faithful servant . . . enter thou into the joy of thy lord."

They taught that no one could know what the reward would be in the case of any particular command fulfilled, and they tended to the view that the giving of the reward would be deferred to the future life. But so far as this life was concerned, then the reward was the sense of inward peace and joy felt by the man who had set himself to do the will of God and had done it.

But this was not the only conclusion which the Pharisees drew from their study of obedience to the divine will. By the act of conscious intentional fulfilling of a precept, as an act of service to God, a man makes a difference not merely in his condition but also in his character. On any given occasion when the opportunity of fulfilling a precept is before him, he can either obey or disobey or remain neutral. If he obeys, he has made a definite assertion of his will and personality on the side of God, he is obviously more pleasing to God than if he had disobeyed or done nothing. His character has acquired a quality which it did not possess before. Something has been added to it, and that " something added " is what is meant by merit, in the Pharisaic teaching. But it should be observed that the term is only used in reference to the man's own share in the act of obedience. He exerted his will, but God helped him to do what was done. The " something added " to his character as a moral agent is the result of his own effort, and would not have come without it. The act of obedience was done, and the result, the " something added," did follow. That was a fact which could be known like any other fact. But it was the help of God which enabled him to perform the act. He acquired merit, *i.e.* the "something added," and he remained humble; a combination which only seems a paradox (or perhaps an untruth) to those who have not understood the real mind of the Pharisees. Self-righteousness was not their spiritual vice, if their own literature, and especially the Jewish liturgy, is to be taken as evidence. There is no other evidence to set against it, except the criticism of the mere onlooker.

We have so far considered the relation between God and man as it would be if the conditions on the human side were completely fulfilled. There would in that case be perfect harmony between them. But actual experience shows that this is far from being the case. When the will of God is disobeyed the harmony is broken, the relation between man and God is interrupted; and the act by which this is brought about is what is meant by Sin, on Pharisaic lines. In a conception of religion where the doing of the divine will was placed first, before everything else, it is evident that sin, as the failure in that respect, must become of tremendous importance. Sin was the act of going against the divine will, whether intentionally or even unintentionally, and the effect of it was to break the harmony which did exist or ought to exist between man and God. The act of disobedience having been done could not be undone, and if there were no way of escape, the position of the sinner would be desperate. The only way by which the broken harmony could be restored, the interrupted relation between man and God resumed, was by means of repentance, expressed in Hebrew by a word (*teshubah*) which means " turning back." The sinner who had by sinning turned away from God, by repenting turns back to him again, and is met by the divine forgiveness. The release of a sinner, on Pharisaic lines, is not by the payment of a debt, whether by the debtor himself or by some one on his behalf; it is by his own intentional act in turning to God and casting himself on the divine mercy. And that mercy is freely exercised in forgiveness, for which there is no claim, and for which the sincere penitent never makes any claim. Forgiveness was in the power of God alone ; and that was why the Pharisees asked : " Who can forgive sins but one, even God ? " (Mark ii. 7).

Sin, forgiveness and repentance fill a great place in the teaching of the Pharisees, as recorded in their literature They held that repentance was always possible, and that if it were sincere God would always forgive. They never had any notion of an Unpardonable Sin ; and the ascription to Jesus of teaching to that effect rests on nothing more than the misunderstanding of a not uncommon Hebrew phrase. Neither did the Pharisees draw from their conception of sin the conclusion which was drawn by Paul, to the effect that a man who was guilty of even one sin was bound by fetters which he could not break, and from which there was no release by anything he could do. They were quite aware that the Torah, or as Paul would call it the Law, could not set the sinner free. But that did not trouble them (if they ever thought about it), because that was not the function of the Torah.

They did not seek for any indirect release, but taught the sinner to turn back to God as he had turned away from him, and God would forgive him. That was the sure way and the only way. Whatever Paul may have learned of Pharisaic theology when he sat at the feet of Gamaliel, he certainly did not learn his doctrine of sin and forgiveness, not merely because it involved Christ, but also because it was fundamentally different from anything ever taught by Pharisees or any other Jews.

Sin, in the view of the Pharisees, always means individual sin; it does not mean the general corruption of human nature, as shown in mankind as a whole. They were perfectly well aware of the evil in the world, and no less horrified at the appalling extent of it than Paul or any other Christian teacher. But they accounted for it in a different, and less artificial, way. In every human being there were, as explained above, the two impulses, one towards good and the other towards evil. The evil impulse was the means by which temptation became effective, and the only means of resisting it was the help of God, sought and obtained. Now the mass of mankind had not the knowledge of God which would enable them to seek his help, or had that knowledge only imperfectly and to a small extent. Hence the evil impulse, acting through countless lives and throughout the ages, was sufficient to bring about the moral chaos of the world, both Jew and Gentile. The only remedy for this, on Pharisaic lines, was the slow working of the knowledge and the influence of God, as more and more were brought to that knowledge and learned to own that influence. There was no place and no need, on these lines, for any dramatic doctrine of Fall and Redemption, whether with or without a special divine agent to effect it. The sin of Adam was a sin, and not without its consequences for his posterity ; but it did not carry with it the monstrous corollary that all his descendants lay under the wrath of God for what he had done.

The foregoing survey of the Pharisaic ideas as to the relation between God and man needs to be completed by showing what beliefs were held in regard to the future, whether of the race or the individual. To this final survey we now proceed.

It is characteristic of Judaism in general, and Pharisaism in particular, to look forward and to hope. None of the other pre-Christian religions could do this ; and the hope which Christianity cherished was to a large extent expressed in terms already familiar in Judaism. The kingdom of God (or Heaven), the coming of the Messiah, the resurrection of the dead, were vital elements in Pharisaic belief ; and through them the hope that inspired Judaism assumed its chief form, while all three were taken over into Christian belief.

Of the three the most fundamental is the kingdom of God. When once that concept assumed clear and definite shape in the Jewish mind it never afterwards lost it, and even before it became clear it was virtually implied. The belief in the coming of the Messiah was subject to variations both of form and intensity. The ideal future was pictured sometimes with and sometimes without a personal Messiah. The belief in the resurrection of the dead finds scarcely any place in the older Scripture, and then only in the Book of Daniel, one of the latest books to be included. It is characteristic of Pharisaic Judaism to a degree not shared by the other two.

The kingdom of God, or of Heaven, is a phrase of purely Jewish origin and meaning. There is no difference between the meaning of the one form of words and that of the other. It arose simply from the desire to avoid using the word God (see above, on the names for God, p. 90). The phrase itself obviously originated in the belief in God as king, a belief which can be traced far back in the religion of Israel. But the exact meaning of the phrase is not easy to define, or rather it seems to lend itself now to one and now to another of several different interpretations. The ambiguity lies in the word " kingdom," and in the Hebrew word (*malkuth*) so translated. It is impossible now to change the usage of centuries, both Jewish and Christian. But the root meaning of the phrase would be better brought out if instead of " kingdom " the word " kingship " were used. What is intended is the rule of God in the heart of man, God owned by man as sovereign Lord. When it is said in the famous words (Deut. vi. 4, 5), " Hear, O Israel, the Lord our God, the Lord is one; and thou shalt love the Lord thy God with all thy heart and with all thy soul and with all thy might," that is to own the kingship of God. And in Jewish usage, when a man repeats those words with entire assent and self-devotion he is said to take on himself the " yoke of the kingdom " (kingship). The words quoted from Deut. vi. are known to Jews by the name of the " Shema," from the first word in Hebrew which means " hear." When reference is made to the Shema (or Shemang) in books and stories dealing with Jewish subjects, the text just quoted is what is meant.   If everything else were stripped away, the Shema would remain to express for the Jew the innermost meaning of his religion.   And that is why Jesus recited the words when he was asked, " Which is the greatest commandment in the Law ? " (Mark xii. 29, 30).   To place this first was not an act of originality on his part, but the answer which would instinctively spring to the lips of every Jew.

To own God as king in the manner indicated above was no mere acquiescence in the decrees of a sovereign ; it was to love to the utmost of one's power the holy, good, just, wise, merciful and loving God, and to devote one's whole self to the doing of his will.   To do this is to own the kingship of God in the heart.   Further, it was the constant thought of the Pharisees that while God was of course eternally supreme, as implied in such statements, *e.g.* as " thy kingdom (kingship) is an everlasting kingdom, and thy dominion unto all generations " (Ps. cxlv. 13), yet he was not effectively king unless those over whom he ruled acknowledged his kingship, in the way described.   So that in a sense it depended on man whether God should be effectively king or not.   But the great mass of mankind do not own him as king.   Either they know nothing about him, or they disregard or defy his will, doing evil in various ways.   He would therefore not be in the fullest sense king until all mankind should own him as such by obedience and love. Israel, indeed, did own him as king; yet even Israel, individually, sinned against him from time to time; and God was thus not fully and effectively king even over those whom he had called to be his special witnesses in the world.

Therefore the thought of the kingship of God necessarily involved a future hope, of a time when the present state of imperfect knowledge and service of God should be replaced by a state of complete and universal faithfulness to him; when, as the prophet had said, " the earth should be filled with the knowledge of the Lord as the waters cover the sea" (Isa. xi. 9). Accordingly, while the kingdom (kingship) of God was already in being in regard to those who did own his rule in the heart, it was still future in regard to those who did not. The kingship of God, which began by being a factor, so to speak, in the life of the soul, acquired the meaning of a state of society, a kingdom, whose extent could be thought of as eventually including all the earth and the inhabitants thereof. It stood for the ideal of collective human life on the earth, to be realised some time, though only God knew when that time should be. In this sense it was possible to speak of the establishing of the kingdom, as an event to be hoped for, and, in the same sense, to pray that the kingdom might come. Until it did come, which would be when it should please God and not before, it was the duty of every faithful son and servant of God to work for the coming of the kingdom. Apart from special action on the part of God, the coming of the kingdom was a gradual process, depending on the faithful services of those who knew him. To make him known in the world was the special task for which Israel had been chosen ; a hard service, as Israel has found all through its history.

The kingdom of Heaven, when and so far as it is established, implies a perfect state of social life. It is not, in essence, concerned with any political or ecclesiastical institutions. Monarchy or priesthood or the absence of them would be quite compatible with the kingdom of God. All that is essential is that all men, under whatever conditions of social life, should own the kingship of God as before described. Of course this would involve the removal of all injustice, oppression, hatred, cruelty, strife and selfishness in every form, because these are incompatible with love to God.

But this truth could be, and was, read in the reverse order, viz. that to remove injustice, oppression, etc., was the necessary prelude to the coming of the kingdom, instead of being its accompaniment or its consequence. Here enters the belief in the coming of the Messiah, which formed the point of attachment for whatever nationalist ideas gathered round the thought of the kingdom of God. More will be said about the Messianic hope when we come to deal with the religious beliefs of the Zealots ; at present we are concerned with the Pharisees.

The word Messiah (Mashiah) means " anointed," and is a shortened form of the phrase " The Lord's Anointed," as used already in the older Scriptures. The word " Christ " (Christos) is the Greek rendering of the Aramaic word. " Christ " has become

by long usage virtually a proper name, applied to
Jesus. But originally it was a title, not a name, as
may be seen in Luke ii. 26. " Messiah " never
became a proper name. It is incorrect to speak of
" Messiah " as denoting a person. It should always
be " The Messiah." The person so designated
was expected to establish the kingdom of God upon
earth; but the hope which looked forward to that
" far-off divine event " did not always associate
with it the expectation of a personal Messiah. At
least this variation is found in the prophetic writings,
which were the source of the belief. In the New
Testament period it was the general belief of all
Jews, unless perhaps the Sadducees, that the Messiah
would come, and would set up the kingdom of
God. It was also believed, perhaps generally, that
the prophet Elijah would be the herald of his coming.
He was commonly expected to be of the lineage of
David, and " Son of David " is the most usual title
given to him, other than " the Messiah " or " the
King Messiah." If the title " Son of Man " was
ever used as the equivalent of " the Messiah," such
use was not common ; and, whatever might be the
case with the Apocalyptic writers, who on the whole
represented Zealot ideas, the use of the term " Son
of Man " to denote the Messiah was not adopted
by the Pharisees.

The Messiah was expected, first and foremost,
to deliver Israel from the yoke of oppression, since
without such deliverance the kingdom of God could
not become a reality. And, obviously, this deliverance would be by sudden act, when it should please
God to send the Messiah, and not by the slow

process of spiritual and moral purification. But it was one of the fixed points of Pharisaic belief that the Messiah would not come nor the kingdom be established until the people had made themselves fit for it by repentance. This is why the call to repentance was associated with the announcement that the kingdom of God is at hand, in the preaching of John the Baptist and of Jesus. And because the Pharisees insisted on this preparation of repentance they would not countenance any attempts to bring the kingdom by violence, as the Zealots were eager to do. This is the fundamental cleavage between the Pharisees and the Zealots, and it is a good deal deeper than is usually supposed. The Messiah, when he did come, would reign, as David had reigned, an earthly king over an earthly kingdom, and would do so not in his own name but as the appointed emissary from God ; and God alone would be really and truly king, since he would then be owned in all the hearts of men. For the Messiah would reign on earth without a rival after he had overthrown the oppressors and those who knew not God. It should be remembered that here as elsewhere there was not a sharply defined doctrine concerning the Messiah and the kingdom of God on earth. Many vivid or lurid pictures are to be found, especially in the Apocalyptic writings, setting forth the bliss of the righteous and the fate of the wicked when the Messiah should have come. But these are picturesque representations, not formal doctrines, and in any case they are characteristic of the Zealots rather than the Pharisees. On the whole, the Pharisees rested in their belief that God was just, that he would send the Messiah in his own good time, that the kingdom would then be established, that an era of peace and righteousness would be ushered in, and that nothing of all this would come to pass unless the people whom it concerned made themselves ready by repentance. Those are the lines of a simple and severe belief, which needed, for the maintenance of it under the suffering caused by Herod and Roman oppression, a rare degree of self-restraint and of heroic devotion to God on the part of men who in this respect also meant sincerely to take on themselves the yoke of the kingdom, and who did not fail in doing so.

The belief in the Messiah and the Golden Age which his coming was to usher in represented the Jewish hope for the future on its national side. Whatever might come to pass in the days of the Messiah would come to pass upon this earth, and would concern those who should then be living on the earth. It did not relate to a future state of existence in heaven; nor indeed to the dead at all, except so far as they might be revived and brought back again. And while the belief in the Golden Age, with or without the Messiah, was clearly indicated in the older Scriptures, especially the writings of the prophets, there is only a slight trace, and that in the latest writings in the canon, of the belief in the resurrection of the dead. This belief was already fully established by the time the New Testament period was reached, and it was held and taught especially by the Pharisees. No doubt it first came clearly into view amongst them. They were able, by their methods of interpretation, to

find abundant warrant for this belief in all parts of
the Scripture ; but in fact it only arose as the result
of the individualising of religion which, as shown
in the first chapter, was one of the characteristic
features of Judaism after the Exile. For, while
the community as a whole would enjoy the peace
and prosperity of the Messianic Age, and even
though all the dead should be brought to life to
share in it, yet resurrection obviously was an individual process ; and the belief in it was an element
which indicated a change in the current conception
of the fate of those whose earthly life was over.
Formerly, the general belief was that the spirits of
the dead were relegated to a region underground,
Sheol, where they existed in a ghostly fashion with
no hope of any release or change.   How or when
the belief in the resurrection began to take shape in
the Jewish mind can only be guessed ; but it would
seem to be suggested by the thought of the Messianic
Age combined with the thought of those who were
believed to have been worthy to share in it, but
whose lives were ended before that age began.
Especially this would be felt in regard to those
who had died for their religion, as in the Maccabean
times.   Since God is just, must there not be for
these, the dead of olden times, some way of making
up for what they had lost either through no fault
of their own or by their own self-sacrifice ?   This
thought would be all the more insistent as the
teachers of Judaism, following the lead of Ezekiel,
laid more and more stress on the worth of the individual soul, and made religion a personal as well as
a communal concern.

H

The centuries between Ezra and the New Testament period were marked by a deepening and
intensifying of the religious life, at all events in the
minds of those who were most influenced by Pharisaic ideas; and it was in such minds that the idea
of the resurrection of the dead first took shape and
became clear.   In place of the endless and aimless
existence in Sheol, there was the hope that at some
future time the dead would be called to life again.
The time when this would take place would naturally
be the Messianic Age; and the life thus renewed
would be lived on earth.   That is the belief in the
resurrection in its simplest form, and apart from
the imagery used to set it forth.   For here again it
is necessary to bear in mind that there was never
any defined doctrine of the resurrection; the hope
that constituted the substance of it was held with a
tenacity which was never relaxed; but, in presenting
this hope to the imagination of those who cherished
it in their hearts, the teachers who set it forth used
such imagery as they thought suitable, and were
never careful that it should all be consistent.   Instead
of spending time over details, it will be more useful
to note one or two main features which distinguish
the belief with resurrection.

It was not, in its origin, intended to offer an
answer to the question, " What becomes of the
spirits of the departed when they die ? "   Rather,
it was intended to supply a defect in the conception
of the Messianic Age, as indicated above.   But
once the idea was started of a resurrection of the
dead, it could hardly fail to suggest further developments, so as to extend the hope not merely to those

who had been long dead but also to those who were now living. And though it was a hope whose fulfilment would come to pass in the Messianic Age, whenever that might be, it could hardly leave unaffected the question of the immediate fate of the departed after death. Strictly speaking, this latter question is not raised by the belief in the resurrection; but it is certain that in the Judaism which developed and strongly clung to the belief in the resurrection a place was found for a belief that the immediate fate of the departed after death was not on the old lines of Sheol.

It should be noticed that Jewish belief in the future state of the departed took the form of resurrection and not of the immortality of the soul. As has been shown above, in the Jewish view of human nature a man consisted of both body and soul, as being both alike of divine origin. To recall a dead man to life must therefore necessarily mean the restoration of both body and soul; otherwise, the being to whom life was given again would not be a man. On the other hand, the doctrine of the immortality of the soul turns on the idea that body and soul were not associated companions both divine in origin, but that the soul only came to its true life when it was set free at death from its earthly prison. And it is one of the points in which Philo parted company with Judaism that he followed the lead of Plato in taking the line of the immortality of the soul and not that of the resurrection of the whole man.

The Pharisees developed the belief in the resurrection of the dead, and insisted upon it so strongly that they gave a place to this belief side by side with the belief in the divine origin of the Torah, in one of the very few official pronouncements upon questions of belief to be found in their literature. The original reference to the Messianic Age was never abandoned; but alongside of it there came to be a reference to the future life, no longer on earth but in heaven. A belief in a general resurrection, after the reign of the Messiah was over, gave further and fuller meaning to the original hope, the expectation being that at that general resurrection a final sentence would be passed upon the good and the bad which would determine their fate, whether for happiness or punishment. The vision of judgment, in Matt. xxv. 31 fol., is laid out on the lines of such a belief.

The belief in the resurrection of the dead began as a hope, but it came to include also a fear. For, if the dead were to be restored to life not so much to enjoy the Messianic Age but to have judgment passed on them, the prospect was very different from what it had seemed at first, and stirred the imagination and still more the conscience of the believer far more deeply. It is this further development of the belief in the resurrection which held the foremost place in Jewish thought, and gave deepest meaning to Jewish speculation on the hereafter. But it does not exhaust the contents of the expectation of the future. For there are indications to show that a belief existed which affected the immediate future after death of those who departed this life. The parable of Dives and Lazarus implies that in the mind of its author, and presumably of his hearers, there was the belief that the good were at once received into bliss and the bad sent to torment. The terms Paradise (Gan Eden, garden of Eden) and Gehenna (Ge Hinnom, valley of Hinnom) were used to denote the two places or states. The phrase used in the parable, "Abraham's bosom," denotes the former, but is very seldom found in the Pharisaic literature. How far the two terms Paradise and Gehenna in the New Testament period were current as referring to the immediate lot of the departed after death may be open to question; but they were so used, and thus this extension of the belief in the resurrection must be included in the survey. In general it may be said, apart from the details of imagery in which the beliefs on the subject were clothed for the purpose of popular edification, that Jewish, and specifically Pharisaic, belief cherished a deep and strong hope for the future beyond the earthly life, a hope whose deepest root was trust in the justice of God and his care for the individual soul. And this hope, with its corollary of fear, was represented now in one way and now in another, as occasion might suggest or the imaginative insight of the teacher might furnish the means of description.

The foregoing survey includes the main beliefs of the Pharisees as to the grounds and truths of religion; and, so far as the Judaism of the New Testament period is represented by Pharisaism, it shows how the religion of the time before the Exile was taken over and carried on with modification and change of emphasis from and after the time of Ezra. The Pharisees, like all other Jews, inherited not only the older Scriptures but also the religion which had inspired those Scriptures. And of all Jews it was the Pharisees who most seriously studied those Scriptures and strove to fulfil not merely the letter but also the spirit of the religion. Beyond any question, the real vitality of Judaism as a religion is to be found in Pharisaism, and it was owing to the strength of that vitality that other forms of Judaism could exist side by side with it and make some appearance of independent worth. The Sadducees, enjoying the prestige of the Temple, could and did far outshine the Pharisees in worldly position and importance; the Zealots could, and on more than one occasion did, drown with their clamour and put to silence with their violence the counsels of submission to the will of God and of waiting his time which the Pharisees offered as the only hope in dark days of oppression; the Essenes gained a character of unworldly piety as holy recluses by shirking the burden which the rest of their fellow-countrymen either endured or struggled and fought to cast away. The Pharisees survived them all, because the Pharisees more than all the rest had learned the inner meaning of the revelation given to Israel through the ages, and by self-sacrificing devotion set themselves to work out, in their own lives and the lives of those whom they could influence, the religion which was the inspiration of their souls.

CHAPTER IV

NON-PHARISAIC JUDAISM

HOWEVER true it is that Pharisaism represents the strongest element in Judaism, yet it was not the only element; and, so far as the number of its professed adherents is evidence, it accounted for only a small proportion of those whose religion is called Judaism. In this chapter we shall study the other groups, previously named, Essenes, Sadducees, Zealots and Am ha-aretz, in order to show what was the main characteristic of their religion wherein they differed from the Pharisees. Since all of them shared a considerable amount of common ground with the Pharisees, being all alike partakers in the religious inheritance of Israel, it will be possible to indicate the points of difference at no great length, and by reference to the survey of Pharisaism to indicate that these other types of Judaism were not restricted merely to the several points of difference. It must always be remembered that all were Jews and their religion Judaism, while each gave to Judaism a particular interpretation, and emphasised special points.

Of the Essenes it seems hardly necessary to say much more than has already been said in Chapter II. By their own act of withdrawal they stood aloof from the main body of Jews, though they never severed the connexion. But they are of little importance for the history either of Judaism or Christianity, except so far as the mystery which enshrouds them affords a wide field for conjecture, and a plausible ground for tracing their influence in quarters not obviously likely. They are not mentioned in the New Testament; and, though they were actually in existence in that period, their influence is negligible and their importance nil.

The Sadducees held a prominent place in the public life of the Jewish people in the New Testament period, at all events so long as the Temple was yet standing. And of Judaism as religion no survey would be complete without some account of the attitude of the Sadducees towards the national faith. That attitude is described by Josephus in terms which are mainly negative, and the evidence of the New Testament and the Rabbinical literature is to the same effect. All agree in stating that the Sadducees denied the resurrection of the dead, and they are further said to have disbelieved in angels and spirits. That they rejected the oral tradition as applied to the Torah was, as we have seen, the chief ground of their disagreement with the Pharisees. Various other points are mentioned, in regard to law or to ritual, upon which the Sadducees held divergent views. But this very meagre list can hardly cover the whole of the religion of the Sadducees, while yet it is not likely that in every particular except those specified they agreed with the views of the Pharisees. How much is to be supplied beyond what is stated, will depend on the view that is taken, as to whether the Sadducees were a religious sect or a political party.

That they were not a school of philosophy, as
Josephus calls them, is as certain as anything can be.
It is not safe to identify them with the High Priests
and their families, though there was evidently some
connexion between them.   They were more or less
closely associated with the Temple, both in the
administration and the maintenance of the elaborate
system of rites and ceremonies ; and this is shown
by the fact that when the Temple was destroyed the
Sadducees, as a group, disappeared from history.
Moreover, they held a quite definite view as to the
authority of the Torah, as has been already shown.
Now since the Temple service while it lasted was the
principal public expression of the national religion,
the Sadducees, so far as they were associated with
the Temple and more or less responsible for the conduct of the services, must have had some positive
religion, even though they held the negative views
attributed to them.   Moreover, they shared with
all other Jews the common ground of the Torah,
and they could hardly have done so unless they had
accepted the main implications of the Torah, viz.
that there was a God, and that he had revealed his
will to Israel, and that it was the duty of Israel to
carry out his will.   We shall perhaps be not far
wrong if we represent the Sadducees as holding the
ancestral religion mainly as an inheritance and not
as a living reality, being content to walk in the old
ways and keep up the old customs, and to distrust
all innovation, whether of belief or practice.   It is
in accordance with this view that they did nothing
to enlarge the meaning or increase the influence of
the Torah, as the Pharisees did ; so far as is known

there was never any effort on the Sadducean side to provide a body of interpretation or a succession of interpreters of the Torah. If there were Sadducean scribes, their function could hardly have extended further than the making of copies of the written text; for the written text alone had for them any authority. The Sadducees, in short, were conservatives in religion and tended towards mere official formality in its observances; while on the other hand they were the less restrained by any religious scruples from engaging in public affairs which involved some amount of compromise with Gentiles. They were not a limited association, as the Pharisees were, and we may reasonably suppose that, on the general lines suggested above, there was a considerable variety of type among the Sadducees in regard to religion, from the high-and-dry precisian of the old school at the one extreme to the mere worldly unbeliever at the other. Such as they were, the Sadducees had little or no direct influence upon the mass of the people, nor did they seek to have. They made no effort to teach the people, presumably because the thought of doing so never entered their minds. Indirectly, they had a good deal of influence, through the Temple service; and while it is true that in the last century of the existence of the Temple the Pharisees were able to impose their will to a considerable extent upon the priests, in the matter of the ritual, yet the Sadducees were, after all, the persons on whom the maintenance and management of the Temple mainly depended, either as priests or as associated with the great priestly families. And so long as the Temple stood, it filled a great place in the imagination of the people and drew to itself a passionate fervour of loyalty, for all that the Synagogue was strengthening year by year its hold on the Jewish heart and soul.

The present chapter is entitled " non-Pharisaic Judaism," in order to include not merely the Essenes and the Sadducees but also those, whoever they may be, whose views are represented in the extensive literature known as Apocryphal, and more particularly that class of works which is called Apocalyptic. By most scholars these writings, or the greater number of them, are assigned to Pharisaic authors, an opinion plausible indeed, but resting on an acquaintance with the principles of Pharisaism which does not go very far or very deep. Those who really do know the Pharisaic literature, including all the great Jewish scholars, agree in the view that the Apocryphal and Apocalyptic writings represent a type (or types) of Judaism different from the Pharisaic type. This does not imply that there was no common ground between them. Seeing that all rested, necessarily, on the basis of Torah, there could not fail to be a large extent of common ground. It is evident to anyone who reads one or other of the Apocryphal books, and who is also in a position to compare it with the Pharisaic literature, that both deal with much the same concepts of religion, such as have been surveyed in the preceding chapter. The term Judaism is rightly applied to both, but not the term Pharisaism ; because the Apocryphal writings, without exception, are not based upon the conception of Halachah, with all its implications, while Halachah is the key to the whole

Pharisaic conception of religion. Unless it is to be supposed that Pharisees ignored the very principle in virtue of which they were Pharisees at all, it is impossible to assign to them the authorship of writings in which that principle is seldom if ever recognised. The various beliefs which have been described in the previous chapter were taught by the Pharisees as Haggadah, a term fully explained already. Haggadah, in the Pharisaic theory, was the complement of Halachah, and both together were the result of interpreting the Torah. In the Apocryphal literature, the beliefs which formed the subject-matter of the Haggadah were for the most part held, though with variation of emphasis; but they were not held as Haggadah in correlation with Halachah. They were just a body of beliefs, so to speak on their own, such as the development of the old religion of Israel through the centuries had produced in the Jewish mind. It may well be that it was the Pharisees who developed them, following in the steps of Ezra, the early Scribes and the Hasidim, as we have seen. But it was obviously possible for men who did not share in the Pharisaic view as to the interpretation of Torah, nor submit to the discipline which they drew from it, to accept their general religious teaching because it appeared to them good and true. And it was no less possible for thoughtful and earnest men, as the Apocryphal writers doubtless were, to have arrived at their religious beliefs independently of the Pharisees, but for much the same general reasons of history and experience.

The Apocryphal and Apocalyptic writings would

have to be dealt with in any survey of Judaism as a whole, but the study of them is indispensable for the right understanding of the Judaism of the New Testament period. For the time in which most of them were written began about a century before that period and lasted till near its close; and, whatever may have been the effect of these writings on the Judaism which survived, their importance for Christianity is unquestionably great. It is, indeed, only through the attraction which they possessed for Christian teachers that they have been preserved at all. In the Pharisaic literature there is no mention of them, though some trifling amount of Apocalyptic matter is found there; and they never secured a place in the list of books regarded as Holy Scripture by Jews, for that canon, as it is called, was finally fixed under Pharisaic supervision and authority. If these writings were known to the Pharisaic leaders, they were deliberately excluded from the canon; if they were not known, their importance for Judaism could not have been very great.

The Apocryphal books are those usually printed separately as the Old Testament Apocrypha; and the word Apocrypha (literally, "hidden") means that the books in question were not received as Holy Scripture. The Apocalyptic books, of which some are and others are not included in the list of the Apocrypha, derive their name from the fact that their main purpose is to convey religious lessons under the form of a "revelation" (Apocalypsis, "unveiling") of the things that shall come to pass "in the latter days." Some ancient personage— Ezra, Solomon, Baruch, Daniel—is introduced as having been shown visions which a heavenly teacher expounds to him, and which relate to such subjects as the coming of the Messiah, the end of the world, the Last Judgment, the fate of the righteous and the wicked, heaven and hell. These topics are usually referred to by scholars under the general term Eschatology, which means the doctrine of the Last Things. The Apocalyptic writings show a strong family likeness in the form in which they are cast, the imagery employed, and the subjects dealt with ; and, with the exception of the Book of Daniel, which was the earliest and set the fashion of this kind of writing, they show hardly any originality of thought. They are ultimately derived from the writings of the ancient prophets, but though the intention is no doubt admirable, the execution is feeble and tawdry. Such appeal as they make is to the imagination of the reader ; and, while charged with emotion, they lay no heavy burden on the intellect. They are of a kind to be extremely popular and widely read, and it is usually assumed that such was the case. This may be true ; but of direct evidence to show that the Apocalyptic books really were well known and widely read there seems to be little or none. They were mostly written in Hebrew, but are only known in trans-lations, usually Greek. This would point to their circulation in the Diaspora, the countries of Jewish residence outside Palestine, rather than in their native land. If they showed any marked originality, in thought or anything else, it would be natural to regard them as the source of the ideas which would seem to have been fairly generally held, as to

Messianic expectation, the fate of the righteous and the wicked and the like. That such ideas were held, is shown by the influence of the Zealots, and by the fact that any hint of a Messianic movement, as by John the Baptist and by Jesus, at once began to awaken and stimulate popular hopes.

The Apocalyptic literature, if it were known and read at all, would find its chief admirers amongst the Zealots; possibly the writers belonged to that party. Its influence, if it had any, would tend to strengthen the Zealots in their fanaticism, and to inflame their zeal both for good and for evil. And, if there were any wide circulation of Apocalyptic writings amongst the Jewish people in general— the Am ha-aretz—the effect, so far as it went, would be to strengthen the influence of the Zealots and weaken that of the Pharisees, as exerted through the Synagogues. Of what actually went on in Palestine during the New Testament period, as to the diffusion of religious ideas and the actual means of that diffusion, much less is known than would provide a secure foundation for the statements commonly made. The Apocalyptic writings, and in general the rest of the Apocrypha, can be used to show that such and such ideas were held in the period in question, and perhaps that they were usual. But it is well to be cautious in attempting to define the extent of the influence of these writings or the manner in which that influence was exerted. That they represent an element, and even a conspicuous element, in the Judaism of the time may be freely admitted. That their importance for the understanding of Judaism has been enormously exaggerated is hardly open to question. A great Jewish scholar has well said that to regard Apocalyptic as representative of Judaism is as unreasonable as to take Christian Science to be representative of Christianity.

The relation of the Apocryphal and Apocalyptic writings to Judaism as a whole and to Pharisaism in particular will be better understood if we bear in mind that Pharisaism was a discipline, and a very strict discipline. The Halachah was a guide to right action in the conscious serving of God. It was an expansion of " Thou shalt " and " Thou shalt not," as set forth in the Torah. No one could be a Pharisee unless he accepted that discipline and acted in accordance with it. This severe demand is no doubt the reason why the actual number of Pharisees was small when compared with the number of the people as a whole. Along with the Halachah the Pharisees taught the Haggadah, in which were included the religious beliefs described in the previous chapter. By reason of the severe discipline of the Halachah, the easier way in religion was obviously to keep outside the range of the Halachah, and take the beliefs without the discipline. The literature which comprises the Apocryphal and Apocalyptic writings is the expression of this attitude of mind ; and if it was popular it was popular for that reason. It appealed to the imagination of the readers, it gave them religious and moral teaching which is sometimes worthy of Judaism at its best, it gave them ideas about God's dealings with the nations of the world which have been dignified with the name of a philosophy of history. It appealed also to national pride and the desire for vengeance on national enemies and oppressors. It described the fate of the righteous and the wicked in the final judgment, and unfolded a sort of drama in successive scenes, which never failed to excite interest even if it did nothing worse. The contents of these various writings were taken from what might be called the common stock of the religious beliefs which made up Judaism, only combined in various proportions, according as the writer wished to lay stress on the ethical or the eschatological side of his subject, or remained on the general ground of religion. Whether a given book were good, bad or indifferent depended on the writer much more than on his material. For that was, on the whole, the same for all, being what has been called the common stock of religious beliefs already described. The want of originality which marks all the literature under consideration is most noticeable in the Apocalyptic writings, where the same fantastic types of imagery are used over and over again, so that one example may serve for all. The fragments of Apocalypse in the New Testament, *i.e.* the passage in Mark xiii., with its parallels in Matthew and Luke and the Book of Revelation, are all on the general lines of the other Apocalyptic writings, though the details may differ as between one and another. From whatever point of view they are regarded, one is about as good as another.

Now it is true of all these writings that they make no demand on the reader, unless it be that which is needed for the finding out of a riddle. They set before him ideas which are sometimes lofty and

I

sometimes base, and leave to him any application
of them. If he took his religion very seriously he
could find in these writings much to inspire him;
if he were indifferent, he could find pleasure in
contemplating the pictures they spread out before
him. But they brought him under no discipline
either to compel or to restrain, they showed him the
religion of the easier way. Human nature being
what it is, that way was followed by the large majority
of the Jewish people, who flinched from the severity
of the Pharisaic discipline. It is easy to understand
that the Pharisees, as men who did take their religion
in deadly earnest, were held in respect and reverence
by the mass of the people, who could not bring
themselves to follow these austere guides in the
discipline of the Halachah; and it is also easy to
understand that the real driving power, the creative
force in Judaism, was to be found with the Pharisees,
who chose the hard and not the easy way in religion.
And so it is that the non-Pharisaic literature represents, both on its good and on its bad side, the
religious ideas of the large majority of Jews in the
period which it covers, while yet it does not represent
that which was really vital, creative and progressive in
the Judaism of that period. This does not mean that
all who were included in that large majority thought
and believed alike; it means that all drew upon
the common stock of ideas and beliefs, and made
whatever use of it, little or much, wise or foolish,
earnest or frivolous, that each might feel disposed
to make. While yet it was the Pharisees, with
their intense concern for making religion a reality,

who kept the Judaism of the whole people alive and able to fulfil its purpose.

We are now in a position to understand the religion of the Zealots and that of the Am ha-aretz, the undefined mass of the Jewish people, so far as these are indicated in the non-Pharisaic literature. It will be convenient to deal first with the Zealots, if only because they were a defined party with a conscious purpose and not a mere collection of various types. The rise of the Zealot party has been described above (pp. 65–71), and it has there been shown that they were primarily a religious rather than a political party. It was, of course, oppression which first drove them into rebellion; but it was oppression as a wrong done to the national religion which provided their keenest weapon. They could make an appeal to which no Jew could be wholly indifferent, especially when enforced by means which made indifference dangerous. Under cover of the religious appeal there was room for social and economic wrongs to find utterance and to increase the desire for vengeance on the nation's enemies. Also there was room under cover of the religious appeal for mere lawless brutality to find its opportunity, as was abundantly shown in the later stages of the two great wars, under Vespasian and under Hadrian. But the root of it all was religion, in the form of religious fanaticism; and the contents of that religion were those elements in the common stock of Judaism which lent themselves to nationalist pride and hatred of Gentiles. These elements are abundantly expressed in the

Apocalyptic writings; and whether those writings were the cause or the effect of the Zealot fanaticism, they were very closely in keeping with it, and some connexion between the two can scarcely be denied. Whether there were writers amongst the members of a party who were noted for their use of the dagger rather than the pen may be open to question. But, whoever wrote the Apocalyptic books, it was the Zealots to whom their message came most directly home, and who did most to translate their words into deeds. They found in those writings not a demand to submit to a discipline such as the Pharisees sought to enforce, but an appeal to imagination and passion, religious zeal, the spirit of martyrdom, the challenge to fight to the death for the Torah and the one only rightful king of Israel, to serve him to the last drop of their blood—and that of their enemies as well. Round these main ideas the contents of Zealot religion would naturally group themselves, belief in the God of Israel, to whom all the so-called gods of the nations were enemies, belief in the holy and divine Torah as the revelation which he had given to Israel and to no other nation on earth, belief in Israel as the Chosen People to whom God would grant final victory over all their enemies, belief in the Messiah who would lead them to victory and execute God's vengeance on the heathen, belief in the kingdom of God on earth as the result of that victory, belief in the final prosperity of the righteous and the destruction of the wicked, as the fitting close of the great drama. The other elements in the common stock of Judaism were more or less in abeyance, not denied but not put forward. The

Zealots were not out to interpret the Torah into a strict discipline and an informal theology, like the Pharisees, nor to combine allegiance to the Torah with worldly policy, like the Sadducees, but to do for its defence what neither the one nor the other could be roused to do. The religion of the Zealots was Judaism, but Judaism ablaze with passion, making of the Torah a battle cry, and inspired by the thought that the " Lord is a man of war."

There remains to be considered, and if possible to be described, the religion of the Am ha-aretz, the undefined mass of the Jewish population. To do this is difficult because that religion never found direct utterance in any literature, also because it is not, on the face of it, probable that that religion was all of one type. Considering that the Am ha-aretz included people of all social ranks and economic status, rich and poor, merchant and artisan, capitalist and labourer, freeman and slave, town-dweller and country-dweller, tax-collector and tax-payer, it is evident that while all were Jews and their religion properly called Judaism, they would not all mean the same thing by it. In the absence of direct evidence, which would illustrate the variety of forms in which popular Judaism was held in the New Testament period, and always bearing in mind that such variety was probable and almost certain, we can yet form some general conclusions from facts which are known. The leading fact is the existence of the Synagogue, as a centre of religious influence and religious teaching. As an institution to be found in well-nigh every town and village, it was in a position to do what the Temple was wholly unable to do and never attempted to do. The Temple was the official shrine of the national religion, the Holy Place where, in some special manner, God was thought to dwell, and where, at the great festivals, the faithful of Israel could present themselves in their thousands, "before the Lord." Doubtless such pilgrimage counted for much in the popular religion, as a periodical renewal of allegiance to the God of Israel, a religious duty performed at the cost of a good deal of trouble and fatigue, and accompanied by some satisfaction and some pleasure in the rare visit to the capital city. The Synagogue offered no such attraction, but it brought religion home to the people in their everyday life, and taught those who would learn their immediate duty to God and their fellow-men. The Synagogue was, if not the creation of the Pharisees, entirely under their control and management, and the teaching given there was naturally in accordance with their views. There were no Sadducean Synagogues, for the Sadducees never took any measures for the religious teaching of the people. Nor were there any specifically Zealot Synagogues, so far as is known. In times when the Zealots were strong and active, they probably made use of the Synagogues as a means of reaching and rousing their fellow-countrymen. But there was no reason why the Zealots should set up Synagogues of their own, apart from those already in existence, since they were not out to teach but to fight. There is occasional mention of "Synagogues of the Am ha-aretz," which would seem to imply places where the teaching given did not altogether come up to the Pharisaic standard.

Since any one who chose could set up a Synagogue, it is conceivable that here and there some group of persons not prepared to go the whole length of the Pharisaic teaching might set up a Synagogue on more congenial lines. But this is only conjecture, and it is probable that disinclination towards the Pharisaic teaching showed itself rather as indifference than as active dissent.

We may take it that the Synagogue set the standard of the popular Judaism, and that the variety of type referred to above consisted in the varying degree in which the religion taught in the Synagogue was received and practised. Moreover, the influence of the Synagogue was only felt directly by those who attended there. Those who did not were only to some extent influenced by the presence in their midst of what might be called their church-going neighbours. The popular religion may therefore be represented as having its source and centre in the Synagogue, whence its influence extended through the population becoming weaker as it was felt further from its source. There would thus be a gradation from all but pure Pharisaism at the one end to complete indifference at the other, with every variety in between.

It should be remembered that the Jews even in Palestine lived in the midst of Gentiles, and were continually exposed to the influence of non-Jewish thought and practice. In proportion as the influence of the Synagogue declined in strength, that of the Gentile environment would become more effective. The result would be not so much the decay of religion altogether as the mingling of Gentile ideas with Jewish, taking shape in a hybrid religion which lost more and more its right to share in the name of Judaism. Some modern scholars have spent much time in tracing connexions between Jewish and Gentile ideas; but the results of such inquiry, however interesting, have no value for the understanding of Judaism properly so called, they belong only to the borderland where Judaism had already lost nearly all that was characteristic of it. It was not this mongrel religion that could keep Judaism alive, or itself either. The popular religion therefore, so far as it was entitled to be called Judaism, might be described as more or less diluted Pharisaism. Jews who went to Synagogue would hear there such teaching of religious beliefs as has been described above, and in a general way would no doubt assent to it. Such fundamental beliefs as those of the unity of God, the divine revelation of the Torah, the calling of Israel, the coming of the Messiah, could hardly be absent from any type of Judaism which still retained that name. And, on the side of practical observance, the remembrance of the Sabbath day and the rite of circumcision were probably universal, though the Sabbath might be remembered with no great strictness in the manner of keeping it. The elaborate structure of Halachah relating to the Sabbath codified in the Mishnah represents rather the logical development on Pharisaic lines of the theory of the Sabbath, and can hardly be taken as describing the general practice even in the third century A.D. Certainly it cannot be taken as indicating the general practice in the New Testament period. It must be always borne in mind that the leaders of Pharisaism had no means of compelling those who were not in their fellowship to conform to their requirements. The people in general followed the teaching and example of the Pharisees just so far as they were individually disposed, and no further. And the inclination to do so would be much less in the case of those who had given up or had never acquired the habit of attendance at the Synagogue on the Sabbath. These are the ones who are described as " sheep without a shepherd " (Matt. ix. 36). Whether they were many or few is a matter of conjecture. It was these especially to whom Jesus addressed himself; but it is reasonable to suppose that the multitudes who followed him and " hung on his words listening " included most of those who were within hearing and many who came out, being attracted by the fame of him, and not merely just those who were outside the range of the Synagogue.

We have already, in connexion with the Zealots, had occasion to deal with the Apocryphal and Apocalyptic literature, as representing a type of Judaism which was not Pharisaic. It is possible, but very far from certain, that that literature was known to and read by persons who belonged to the Am ha-aretz. The most that can be safely asserted is that the characteristic ideas of the Apocalyptic writings were to some extent familiar to the people in general. This is evident from the fact that the preaching of John the Baptist, and still more the preaching of Jesus, aroused expectations of a kind which was obviously Messianic, whether so intended or not. But Zealot influence is quite enough to account for the spread of such ideas, without assuming a popular knowledge of a literature of whose origin and extent of circulation practically nothing is known. To suppose that Jesus, or any one else, had a private library in which these books were kept and read is a pure assumption, for which nothing that is known of the usages of Jews in the New Testament period affords any support. And even if, as has been supposed, a Synagogue in Capernaum for instance possessed a library where an intelligent inquiring man might go and read, the authorities of that Synagogue, being Pharisees, would take good care that none of the Apocalyptic writings was to be found on its shelves.

Further than what has been suggested it seems hardly possible to go, in indicating the nature of the popular Judaism in the New Testament period. At least it is safer to refrain from positive assertion, either of laxity or rigour, as characteristic of the people in general; and to remember that, from the nature of the case, while there was probably a general likeness in the religion of the Am ha-aretz, without which it could not have remained Judaism, there was no less probably a wide variety in the types represented.

We have now surveyed the Judaism of the New Testament period considered as a body of beliefs, held, with varied emphasis, by certain definite groups or by the general mass of the population, and have traced the connexion of these beliefs with those carried over from the older religion of Israel to the period after the Exile. We have noted the strong lead given by Pharisaism, and the response or resistance offered to that lead by the other elements in the population. We can therefore, to some extent, form a conception of what Judaism was and what it meant to those who held it, in the period with which we are concerned. But this needs to be supplemented by a survey of what may be called Judaism in operation, by which is here meant Judaism as expressed in the conduct and actions of different persons, official and private. We read of priests, scribes, doctors of the law, the ruler of the Synagogue, and many others ; and, for the proper understanding of the Judaism of the period, it is needful that we should know who these persons were, what they did, and why they did it, as the consequence of their Judaism. Also, what the ordinary unofficial private individual usually did or might be expected to do, in virtue of his religion. To this inquiry the next chapter will be devoted.

CHAPTER V

In the preceding chapters an account has been given of the contents of Judaism in the New Testament period, its leading principles and main beliefs, according as these were accepted by various sects and parties and by the undefined majority of the people. It is hoped that no important type has been omitted. These various principles and beliefs gave rise to action in many ways, ranging from the elaborate system of the Temple ritual and its administration to the conduct of the private individual, and including midway between the two extremes the institution and management of the Synagogue. This threefold division may serve as a guide in making a survey of practical Judaism in the period with which we are concerned, and it will be convenient to begin with the Temple.

At the opening of the New Testament period the Temple was in its full glory as a far-famed sanctuary. It had recently been rebuilt by Herod the Great, on a scale of gorgeous splendour exceeding anything that had been seen in Jerusalem in earlier times. And while his action in pulling down the old Temple and building the new one might raise some doubts and call forth some disapproval, yet the result was that the national religion, so far as it found expression in the Temple, was housed and its rites were performed with a magnificence unknown before. The Temple was, outwardly at least, the greatest and grandest thing that the Jewish people had to show. Though the actual building was new, and indeed was hardly completed before it was destroyed in A.D. 70, yet it gathered up and enshrined the whole tradition of the national religion, at least as far back as the reign of Solomon. It was one of the " sights " of the then known world, visited by travellers who had no connexion with Judaism, and still more by the large crowds who went up to Jerusalem at the three great festivals in each year. Of this more will be said presently ; it is mentioned here in order to show that the Temple would be more or less familiar, by personal visit or by description, to practically every Jew who was living while it still stood. It was in some sense a national possession, for a contribution of half a shekel * was levied for its support upon every adult Jew (Matt. xvii. 24–27), and there is no evidence that this payment was ever grudged, until, after the destruction of the Temple, the half-shekel was converted into a tax payable to the Roman government. Moreover, though the crowds who thronged the Temple had comparatively little share in the ritual acts, they felt a personal concern for the proper performance of them, and on occasion showed their resentment of an irregularity.

* The shekel at this time was worth perhaps about three shillings. Assuming that the half-shekel was paid by a million persons, which is a reasonable estimate, the annual income of the Temple from this source alone would amount to £75,000.

The Temple services involved a very extensive and elaborate ceremonial, of which one main feature was the sacrifice of animals. A vast number of priests and levites found employment not only in the actual performance of the services, but also in the care and upkeep and menial offices of the buildings and their equipment. The sacred purpose for which the whole institution existed was doubtless not entirely forgotten, but it tended to be lost sight of amid the mass of administrative detail and the pressure of vested interests. For good and for evil the Temple system was an ancient institution whose high renown did not suffice to keep it clear from corruption, and whose official sanctity was no protection against the degradation of unspiritual custom.

Mention is made in all four Gospels, in connexion with the incident known as the cleansing of the Temple, of the traffic in sheep and cattle, the changing of money, etc., which was carried on to such an extent as to call forth the severe rebuke of Jesus. The fact of such traffic is undeniable, and, from the point of view of a purely spiritual religion, highly objectionable; but in order to judge it rightly it should not be taken out of its context, as if it were a solitary act. It formed part of the whole system of sacrifice and offering for which the Temple existed, the intention being that every worshipper should be able to provide himself with the proper means of sacrifice on the spot where it was wanted. The money-changers were there to enable the worshipper to obtain, in exchange for his own local currency, whatever it might be, the standard coin in which

alone the Temple tax might be paid. In theory, at
all events, these operations were not carried on for
private profit, as if they were merely commercial;
they were managed by priests, and for the benefit
partly of the Temple, partly of the worshippers.
Moreover, they were carried on not in the Temple
itself but in the outer enclosure, known as the
Mount of the House, or the Court of the Gentiles,
which was so far from being sacred that Gentiles
might freely enter there. The need for caution in
judging and condemning the traffic in the Temple
is shown by the fact that the sacrifices themselves,
though to modern ideas far more repulsive, called
forth no protest from Jesus or from any one else.
The great altar streamed with the blood of the
victims slain in hundreds and sometimes in thousands, the air was filled with the stench of burning
flesh, the priests must have looked like butchers,
though they did not do the actual killing. The
whole Court of the Priests became a shambles,
and imagination revolts from the picture which a
knowledge of the facts sets before it. To the
modern mind it is well-nigh inconceivable that any
worship, unless that of Moloch, could find expression
through such gross and brutal rites. Yet it did,
and that not alone in Jerusalem but in well-nigh
every temple throughout the then known world.
Animal sacrifice was the almost universal practice;
and the frequent accompaniment of rites which did
not involve bloodshed in no way mitigated the
horror of those which did. All this was so much
the general practice that it called forth no protest or
even remark; and, while the Temple in Jerusalem

could show on how great a scale animal sacrifices could be offered, that was a matter of conscious pride on the part of the nation whose Temple it was. It seems strange to reflect that prayer was offered and psalms were sung in the intervals of the sacred slaughter; but so it was, and those who prayed and those who sang, and those whose hands were stained with blood, "up to the elbows" as the Talmud says somewhere, were more or less the same persons. It was surely well for humanity when the Temple made way for the Synagogue and the Christian Church; but the fact remains and must be admitted, that the religion which produced the Synagogue, and indirectly the Christian Church, had one of its main roots in the Temple service.

For the performance of the service and the discharge of the duties incidental to the management and upkeep of the Temple an immense number of priests and levites was necessary. At the head of all was the High Priest, whose office was in earlier times probably hereditary; but, from the time of Herod down to the fall of the Temple, subject to frequent and sudden change, according to the caprice of the king or the Roman governor, as the case might be. So frequent were the changes, that there might be, at a given time, several men who had held the office of High Priest. These are included amongst those who are called, in the Gospels, the Chief Priests, though the term probably refers also to leading members of their family and kindred. These lived for the most part in Jerusalem, as being the centre of affairs. The rank and

file of the priests, however, were distributed over
the whole country.   They were divided into twenty-
four sets, and each set went on duty in the Temple
for a week at a time.   A " set " included levites as
well as priests, and was sufficiently numerous to
provide, during its term of service, the whole staff
of the Temple with the exception, of course, of the
permanent high officials.   The priest and the levite
in Luke x. 31–32 were returning home to Jericho
after their week's term of duty.   Jericho is said to
have contained enough priests to furnish a complete
" set " by itself.   Attached to each "set " was a company of men resident in Jerusalem, who attended at
the Temple services, as representatives of the people
in general, whenever their " set " was on duty.   Of
the High Priests mentioned or referred to in the
New Testament Annas and Caiaphas are mentioned together, Luke iii. 2 ; John xviii. 13, 24 ;
Acts iv. 6.   Annas (= Hanan) was the father-in-
law of Caiaphas.   In Luke iii. 2, Caiaphas (Joseph
Caiapha) was the actual officiating High Priest,
and he held the office from A.D. 18–36 approx. ;
but Annas was still called High Priest, though no
longer in office, in accordance with the usage of the
time, mentioned above.   Ananias (Hananiah), the
High Priest before whom Paul was accused (Acts
xxiii. 2), held office from A.D. 47–59 approx.   John
and Alexander (Acts iv. 6) never actually held
office, but were only members of one or other of the
chief priestly families.   The Captain of the Temple
(called the chief captain, Acts xxi. 31) was not a
priest nor a Jew, but the commandant of the Roman
garrison stationed in the fortress overlooking the

K

Temple. There was an officer who was head of the Temple police, probably a priest; but he is not mentioned in the New Testament.

It is hardly necessary to give a detailed description of the ritual of the Temple services, ordinary or special; but some of the allusions to the Temple to be found in the New Testament may be noticed. The stories told in Luke ii. have the Temple for their background. The infant Jesus is said to have been presented there by his parents, who brought the usual offerings in connexion with the redemption of the first-born; the offerings being such as were made by poor persons. Of Simeon and Anna who are mentioned in connexion with this incident nothing is known. They may be imaginary figures. The story told in the same chapter of the boy Jesus in the Temple in the midst of the doctors may or may not be historical, but it was told by one who knew something of what was done in the Temple, particularly at the great festivals. Within the Temple, in addition to the sacrifices and the priests and the whole ritual system, there was a Synagogue, also three Courts of Justice (*Beth Din*) and a kind of college (*beth ha-midrash*) where the Torah was studied and expounded by the learned men. Usually such study was carried on in the college, presumably some room in the Temple building, perhaps the Synagogue. But occasionally, when the number of hearers was large, the whole company adjourned to the courtyard outside, and the teacher sat in the shadow while his audience stood or sat round him. On the occasion of the great festivals it was usual to explain thus publicly the precepts relating to the particular festival. But the teaching was not confined to this subject, nor was it given only as the discourse of a single teacher. Any person present might ask questions, and such questioning would be treated not as a rude interruption, but as a welcome sign of interest. There is therefore nothing in the story about Jesus in the Temple which is out of accord with the known practice of the time. It would be quite easy for him to join the crowd of listeners round the teachers ; and if, being interested, he began to ask questions no one would rebuke him or bid him be silent. These grave " doctors of the law " would be only too pleased that a boy should show so much interest and intelligence, instead of running off to see the sights. There is no ground for making a great matter of this incident, as if it were something unheard of. What was exceptional was not the incident but the boy. The story, being found only in one Gospel, is by many scholars put aside as unhistorical ; but there is nothing on the face of it to prove it such ; and any one who knew as much as the story implies would, if his object were to glorify Jesus, have known that he must shape his story differently. Rightly understood, the incident is so slight and ordinary that no one would have troubled to invent it, and it may very well be a chance recollection of the boyhood of Jesus. No doubt the Evangelist put it in because he thought it tended to the exaltation of Jesus.

A word may here be said as to the crowds who went up to Jerusalem at the three great festivals. In theory every male Jew above the age of twelve was bound to " appear before the Lord " three times in the year; and possibly while the Jewish people dwelt within the limits of the Holy Land the practice was in fairly close accordance with the theory. But, in the New Testament period, when Jews were to be found in every country of the then known world, it was impossible for the theory to be put in practice. Doubtless every country was represented in the yearly pilgrimage, but certainly not every adult Jew made the journey. Much depended, naturally, on the distance from Jerusalem. And, after all, no one was or could be compelled to make the journey. Of the actual number of pilgrims present in Jerusalem at the great festivals nothing is known with certainty. It is told in the Talmud, and also by Josephus, that King Agrippa II, shortly before the siege of Jerusalem, ordered a calculation to be made of the number present at the Passover festival by counting the number of lambs offered and killed in the Temple. The total works out at some 12 million persons (Talmud) or $2\frac{1}{2}$ millions (Josephus). That either of these numbers should be correct is physically impossible, having regard to the available space in the Temple and in the city. The Talmud contains, however, a statement on much more sober lines, from which it follows that the number of persons at a normal Passover festival was from ten to fifteen thousand. It could not have been much more.* On one occasion a man was killed in the crush in the Temple,

* I owe this calculation to the Russian scholar Chwolson; see his " Das letzte Passamahl Christi," 1908, p. 49 fol.

and that was noted as a rare occurrence. This goes to show that the number present could not have been more than a few thousands.

The Temple proper stood within the wide enclosure of the Court of the Gentiles, otherwise known as the Mount of the House. This enclosure was surrounded, within its boundary wall, by a cloister or arcade supported on pillars and opening on to the courtyard. This cloister is what is known as Solomon's Porch (Acts iii. 11), though the word porch does not convey the meaning intended. The Beautiful Gate mentioned in the same chapter (Acts iii. 2, 10) was probably the gate leading from the Court of the Gentiles into the Temple proper. It led to the first of three courts, one behind the other, known respectively as the Court of the Women, the Court of Israel and the Court of the Priests. The first was called the Court of the Women because it was the only one of the three to which women had access, except for special purposes. It follows that Jews of both sexes and all ages could gather in the Court of the Women, and it was the part of the Temple in most constant and general use. It was here that people went for private prayer, like the Pharisee and the Publican (Luke xviii. 10), or Peter and John (Acts iii. 1). There could be little or no privacy in a great court, measuring some 200 feet square and usually filled with people coming and going; but that would be no hindrance to oriental devotion. It was in this court that the crowds gathered on any occasion of excitement, as when the people shouted Hosanna to the Son of David on the

entrance of Jesus into the Temple (Matt. xxi. 14 fol.).
It was here that he sat daily and taught (Matt. xxvi.
55). It was here also that Paul was assailed by the
crowd (Acts xxi. 28) on the suspicion that he had
brought Gentiles into the Temple where no Gentile
might come.

A further point of interest about the Court of the
Women calls for fuller notice. As this court was
the most usual resort for Jews, it was the place chosen
for putting the chests or collecting-boxes intended
to receive the contributions of the worshippers.
There were thirteen of these chests, and they were
placed probably in the pillared arcade which surrounded the court, but in any case in such a
position that any one, if he chose, could watch those
who put in money, and even see whether it was much
or little, gold or silver or copper. This is the scene
of the story of the Widow's Mite (Mark xii. 41–44)
and sufficiently explains what is there told. These
thirteen money chests were shaped like trumpets,
being narrow above and wider below, and they were
in fact called trumpets. They were the Treasury
into which gifts were cast; and the amounts so
collected were stored in other parts of the Temple
building and used for various purposes connected
with the enormous expense of the upkeep and
administration and also for charity. Now there was
in the Temple building a certain room called the
Chamber of the Silent. This also was used for
storing gifts of money; but the peculiarity of it was
that any one who wished to do so might go there
secretly and leave his gift unobserved. And in

like manner, charity was dispensed from that room secretly, in order that those who received it might not have their poverty exposed to public notice.

Now it is said in the Sermon on the Mount (Matt. vi. 2), " When therefore thou doest alms, sound not a trumpet before thee as the hypocrites do in the synagogues and in the streets . . . but when thou doest alms, let not thy left hand know what thy right hand doeth," etc. Of any actual blowing of a trumpet, in the Synagogue or anywhere else as an accompaniment of almsgiving, there is no trace whatever in Jewish literature, and it is obviously out of the question. Also, there was no actual giving of alms in the Synagogue. But I suggest that the clue to the passage about open and secret almsgiving is afforded by the " Trumpets " and the " Chamber of the Silent " described above; and that in effect, Jesus said, " When thou doest alms, put not thy gift into the ' Trumpets,' but rather go to the ' Chamber of the Silent,' where no one will see or know what thou givest." The reference to the Synagogues and the streets may well have come in from the following verse, about prayer. The thought based on the usage of the Temple could, of course, be figuratively extended to almsgiving in general.

Closely associated with the Temple, though in strictness not forming part of its organisation, was the Assembly referred to in the Gospels and Acts under the name of the Council. This rather colourless word represents the Hebrew word

Sanhedrin,* which ought to have been retained, because the name denoted a particular assembly, and not just any and every council. The Greek word " Synedrion," translated by " Council," occurs seventeen times in the New Testament in this special meaning, and the reference is to the Supreme Council under the presidency of the High Priest. During most of the period from its institution, probably in 190 B.C. or thereabouts, down to the time of Herod, the Sanhedrin under the High Priest had a large share in the government for all purposes, civil, political, judicial and religious. It did not cease to exist until the fall of Jerusalem in A.D. 70; but under Herod nearly all its authority was taken away and exercised by the king, and the Romans only allowed it to function under considerable restriction. So long as it lasted, however, the Sanhedrin was nominally the chief (Assembly of State;) and, if its political importance had sunk almost to nothing, it retained a good deal of its judicial power. In criminal cases it could pass a sentence of death, though it could not proceed to execution. For the death penalty the permission of the Roman governor had to be obtained; or rather, if the sentence were confirmed, it was carried out by the governor's orders and by his officers. The Sanhedrin was supposed to consist of seventy members exclusive of the High Priest; but it is

* The word is really the Greek " _synedrion_ " adapted to Hebrew use. The form " Sanhedrim," as it is often written, is incorrect; the termination " im " is taken to be the usual Hebrew plural, but there is no plural in the case. Sanhĕdrin should have the accent on the middle syllable.

not known whether this represents the actual facts. All that can be said with safety is that it included the leading men of the time, especially those most closely associated with the High Priest, but also " doctors of the Law " (of whom more will be said presently) and influential laymen. Thus Sadducees and Pharisees were both included, though the latter were not in a majority until the last few years before the fall of Jerusalem.

It is believed that the foregoing account is substantially correct; but it should be added that there are many intricate problems connected with the real constitution of the Sanhedrin, due to a confusion between that body and a tribunal called in the Talmud the Great Beth Din (law court). The discussion of the relation between these two is not necessary for the present purpose. It is only mentioned because many who have written about the Sanhedrin have based their accounts on the Talmudic evidence, which is quite valid and very valuable, but refers to an assembly not identical with the actual Sanhedrin, though it became its successor after the fall of Jerusalem. It is probable that the name Sanhedrin was sometimes applied in actual usage to this other body, the Great Beth Din, which was entirely Pharisaic and composed of " doctors of the law." This latter body does not appear in the New Testament, but traces of the name Sanhedrin, apart from those already referred to, can be found there. For, in addition to the Great Sanhedrin just described, there were smaller assemblies which served as local tribunals, and these were also called by the name of Sanhedrin. They consisted either of twenty-three members or of seven (or in some cases three), the former being set up in towns of more than 120 inhabitants, the latter in villages with less than that number.   Naturally, the powers of the smaller courts were more restricted than those of the larger ; and there was an appeal from the lower to the higher, and in the last resort to the Great Beth Din in Jerusalem.   When it is said (Matt. x. 17) " They will deliver you up to councils " the reference is to the local tribunals just mentioned.   In the Temple the Great Beth Din met in what was known as the " Hall of Hewn Stone," and two of the smaller tribunals also met within the Temple precincts.   Where the Sanhedrin met is not quite certain, but it was somewhere near the altar.   There is reason to suppose that in the last years of the Temple, when the Pharisees had control, the Sanhedrin was forced to leave the Temple premises and meet on the secular ground of the city. That it did not always meet in the Temple is shown by the accounts of the trial of Jesus, which refer to a meeting in the house of the High Priest (Mark xiv. 53), who certainly did not live in the Temple, though he had a private room there.   The trial of Jesus as described in the Gospels would not be in accordance with the procedure laid down in the Talmud, but that is because the Talmud had in view the Great Beth Din which it identified, mistakenly, with the Sanhedrin as it existed while the Temple yet stood. Whether the trial of Jesus was strictly in accordance with the procedure of the actual Sanhedrin cannot be determined ; and it is reasonable to suppose that the High Priest and his associates were more

impressed with the need of making an end of their
prisoner than of complying with legal forms. There
were Pharisees on the Sanhedrin, but it was not their
assembly, at all events till long after the death of
Jesus. The Sanhedrin belonged mainly to the
Sadducees, and it was they, and not the Pharisees,
who condemned Jesus to death and handed him
over to Pilate. That the decision was not unanimous
is shown by the example of Joseph of Arimathea
(Luke xxiii. 50), who was a " councillor," *i.e.* a
member of the Sanhedrin, and who "had not
consented to his death."

Having surveyed the Temple as a prominent
factor in the Judaism of the New Testament period,
we may now pass to the consideration of the
Synagogue as an even more important factor. The
transition from the one to the other may be con-
veniently made by way of the persons known as
Scribes and " doctors of the law." For these were
Pharisees, and the Synagogue was entirely Pharisaic,
while yet Scribes and doctors of the law were to some
extent represented in the Sanhedrin which has just
been mentioned. In Acts v. 34 it is said that
" There stood up in the Council a Pharisee named
Gamaliel, a doctor of the law, had in honour of all
the people." This was the Gamaliel at whose feet
Paul said that he had sat as a student. He was,
at the time of the incident described, the leading
Pharisee in Jerusalem, and president of the Great
Beth Din, the exclusively Pharisaic tribunal or court.
Presumably that is the reason why he had a seat in
the Sanhedrin, as being a man too influential to be
left out by the Sadducean leaders. He is called a

" doctor of the law," and thus belonged to a class of persons referred to occasionally in the New Testament. What is really meant by this title would be more clearly understood if it were read as " teacher of the Torah." It has been explained above that the word " Law " is always and everywhere a wrong rendering of the word Torah; and it has been shown at length that the Torah was, especially in the view of the Pharisees, the whole divine revelation contained in the written text of the Pentateuch and the unwritten tradition which alone gave the true interpretation of that text. From the time of Ezra interpretation of the Torah, with a view to the practical application of its teaching, had been a prime necessity; and that necessity has never ceased to be recognised, and provided for, down to the present day. In the New Testament period it was already an institution of long standing that there should be men who devoted their whole lives to the study and exposition of the Torah in order to instruct all whom they could influence in the right way of fulfilling its precepts and receiving its truths. They did this, in the first instance, to pupils, disciples, whom they gathered round them; and each teacher had his own " house of study," *beth ha-midrash*, for the purpose. And further, the teachers conferred together as experts, to give decisions on all questions of Halachah, *i.e.* the practical application of Torah to action and conduct. The various tribunals, *beth din*, described above, were, if not entirely composed of these expert teachers of Torah, certainly led by them; and the Great Beth Din, as the final court of appeal, was undoubtedly a body of experts, the most eminent and experienced teachers of the time. As we have seen, Gamaliel was the president at the date of the incident described in Acts v. 34.

The term " doctor of the law," which is a correct translation of the Greek word used in the New Testament, is not the translation of any Hebrew title, at least not of any in common use. The ancient title, as old as the time of Ezra, was " Scribe " (*Sōpher*); and that title was still used in the New Testament period, though with a clear consciousness that the Scribes of the later time were not quite the same as those who were identified with the Great Synagogue in the age following on Ezra (see above, p. 37). That the term " Scribe" was in use in the New Testament period is evident from the frequent mention of them in the Gospels; but in the Talmud and the cognate literature the chief teachers are not often called by the title of Scribe. The collective name in that literature for the teachers is " the Wise." There was, however, another title that seems to have been coming into use in the time of Jesus, viz. the title " Rabbi " (literally, " my master "); and it is possible that " Rabbi " is equivalent to what the Gospels call " doctor of the law." As " Scribe " and " doctor of the law " are both mentioned, the Evangelists presumably were aware of some distinction of title which they tried to reproduce; and the introduction of " Rabbi " may have helped to restrict the meaning of " Scribe " to what it afterwards became—little more than what might be called an elementary school teacher. In regard to the duties of their office, there is, in the New Testament period, no appreciable difference between " Scribe " and " doctor of the law," or Rabbi. They were the men whose chief business it was to learn and to teach the Torah—in other words, to study it, interpret and apply it. They needed to have a perfect mastery of the text of Scripture, and an expert knowledge of the unwritten tradition, and of the rules of its correct interpretation. But it should be borne in mind that these functions meant to the Pharisee (and the Scribes and Rabbis were all Pharisees), not the legal task of administering a code, but the religious task of making the divine revelation an integral part of life. Whatever, in connexion with the Torah, had this for its object came within the duties of a Scribe, whether it was to write copies of the text of the Pentateuch, or to give decisions as a judge in the Beth Din, or to study and teach Torah in the Beth ha-midrash, or to edify the people in the Synagogue.

On the lines just laid down, the Scribes and " doctors of the law " were the most learned men of their time, and were honoured accordingly. They were not, however, a professional class in the sense in which the term is used nowadays. That is to say, men might be Scribes or Rabbis while following some trade or calling, and many of the most famous teachers in the New Testament period were artisans or tradesmen. In this respect, Paul as a tent-maker was quite a typical Jewish teacher. Any man, in any walk of life, might, if he chose and could give the needful time and strength, devote himself to the study of Torah, and would, when duly proficient, be recognised and acknowledged as a competent teacher, with the title of Rabbi.

In the Gospels the foregoing titles are mentioned in various combinations, thus:—" Scribes and Pharisees " (Matt. xxiii. 2), " the Scribes of the Pharisees " (Mark ii. 16), " Pharisees and doctors of the law " (Luke v. 17), " Chief Priests and Scribes " (Matt. xx. 18), " Elders of the people . . . both Chief Priests and Scribes " (Luke xxii. 66), " Rulers of the Pharisees " (Luke xiv. 1). What has been already said will make it easy to understand the meaning of the different expressions. We will take them in order.

(1) Scribes and Pharisees. This implies both a likeness and a difference. The Pharisees held such views as have been set forth in an earlier chapter, both as regards religion in general and the Torah in particular. The Scribes were those who studied and taught the Torah on Pharisaic lines. A Pharisee was not, however, necessarily a Scribe; and, in theory, a Scribe was not necessarily a Pharisee. He might be an expert teacher and student of Torah, even on Pharisaic lines, while yet remaining outside their organisation. It is even possible that a Scribe should not follow the Pharisaic line in his interpretation of Torah. But, if there were Sadducean Scribes, they could hardly be more than literal copyists of the text of the Pentateuch, because the Sadducees, as already explained, did not elaborate a system of interpretation, as the Pharisees did. There was no Sadducean Halachah, unless by way of denial of the Halachah of the Pharisees. And this

explains the term (2) Scribes of the Pharisees, if the reading in Mark ii. 16 be correct. The term does not seem to occur elsewhere, for Acts xxiii. 9 is not quite the same. (3) " Pharisees and doctors of the law " falls under the same explanation as Scribes and Pharisees, No. 1. (4) Chief Priests and Scribes. When these are mentioned together the reference is usually to the Sanhedrin (see above), because that was the only body which included them both. As a rule, Chief Priests, being mostly Sadducees, would not be naturally associated with Pharisees. And where (5) " Elders of the people . . . both Chief Priests and Scribes " are mentioned together, the explanation is the same. The " Rulers of the Pharisees " (6) probably means such members of the Sanhedrin as were Pharisees ; there was no one whose function it was to rule over Pharisees as such. " Councillor " (Luke xxiii. 50) has already been explained to mean " member of the Sanhedrin." " Lawyer " (Luke x. 25) may mean the same, or merely " Scribe " or " doctor of the law."

The Pharisees in the Gospels are mentioned without any indication of difference between one type and another. But it should be noted that there were, at the beginning of the New Testament period, two eminent teachers, Shammai and Hillel, who, in their teaching, were so far opposed to each other that their disciples were ranged in two groups, known as the House of Hillel and the House of Shammai. Controversy between these two groups extended over many topics and excited considerable warmth of feeling. But both groups were Pharisees, and both were concerned with the right definition of the Halachah. The real controversy was whether the Halachah should be finally decided in accordance with the view of the one party or of the other. The House of Hillel prevailed at last, and the controversy ceased to be acute towards the end of the first century A.D. So far as the difference between the two Houses related to other than minute details of Halachah, it may be said that on the whole the House of Shammai, while not ceasing to be Pharisees, stood nearer to the Zealots than the House of Hillel did, who were always strictly pacifist. In the incident of the tribute money (Matt. xxii. 15 and par.) it was the Pharisees who put the question to Jesus ; and it is conceivable that their intention was not merely to entrap him but to see what he would say upon a matter in regard to which they themselves were divided. If he had answered definitely either for or against the payment of the tribute money, he would have gone contrary to the opinion of one or the other of the two Houses, and so could be accused or disarmed as the case might be.

We may now proceed to the consideration of the Synagogue as an institution, and of the way in which it played its part in the Judaism of the New Testament period. Something has been said already (above, p. 23 fol.) as to the origin and function of the Synagogue, as representing a type of religious thought and practice widely different from that represented by the Temple. It will be unnecessary to dwell further on this side of the subject ; but, as in the case of the Temple, so in the case of the Synagogue, it will be useful to study the references contained in the New Testament to the Synagogue, its services, its officers, etc.

The Synagogue was the organ of the popular Judaism, because it was found in every Jewish centre of population and was organised on demo-cratic non-professional lines. It was a laymen's church, intended and carried on for the purpose of making religion effective in the life of the people. It is worth notice that attendance at the Synagogue was voluntary. Of course such attendance was encouraged and praised; but there was never any definite command on the subject. Obviously there could be none in the Pentateuch; and the Halachah, in dealing with the subject, could only assume that the pious Jew would go to Synagogue. It could not require that he should go. There is no treatise in the Talmud dealing with the subject of the Synagogue, let alone the duty of attendance there. The type of religion represented by and in the Synagogue was Pharisaism, because the Pharisees were the only ones amongst the leaders of Judaism who took thought for the religious instruction of the people in general. If they did not create the Synagogue they developed it with this end in view. The teaching given in the Synagogue was neces-sarily Pharisaic, and such as has been described above (Chapter III. See also pp. 133–138).

A Synagogue was primarily an assembly rather than a building. Of course, a place in which to meet was necessarily implied; but it might be, and often was, a room in a private house set apart for the purpose. A group of not less than ten

adult males could, if they chose, set up a Synagogue
if they could have the use of a room for prayer
and study of Torah. When it is said that in
Jerusalem there were 480 Synagogues, the number
is probably exaggerated, but it may include the
small assemblies in private houses. There were,
however, larger buildings set apart for the purpose
of a Synagogue and intended to be used by a considerable number of people. In Nazareth, for
instance, the Synagogue mentioned in Luke iv.
would seem to have been the place of meeting for
the whole village. Some of the larger towns may
have had several Synagogues. If Capernaum be
rightly identified with the modern Tell Hum, the
ruin of a large and handsome building bears witness to what the chief Synagogue of that town was
like. Probably the larger Synagogues followed the
model of the Roman basilica in their general plan ;
but there was no one type to which conformity was
required, nor was there any position or direction,
as *e.g.* lying east and west, in which a Synagogue
must be built. The one essential was a place of
meeting large enough to accommodate those who
would habitually make use of it. The usual Hebrew
name for a Synagogue means simply " meeting-
house."

The internal arrangements were very simple.
The only indispensable piece of furniture was the
Ark, a wooden chest in which the Scrolls of the
Torah and of the prophets were kept. This was
movable, and on solemn occasions, *e.g.* a public
fast day, could be carried in procession through the
streets. The Ark was placed in a conspicuous

position at the end of the room, and there were steps leading up to it. There was also, close by the Ark, a raised platform from which some of the prayers were recited and the Scripture read. A table or reading-desk was usually provided, but not always. The worshippers for the most part sat on the floor on mats, but there were sometimes seats against the wall, and there were always seats for the Ruler of the Synagogue (see below), the Elders, the learned men, and any persons to whom it was desired to show special honour. These " chief seats in the Synagogue " (Matt. xxiii. 6) were placed so that those who sat in them faced the congregation and had their backs to the Ark ; they were probably arranged on the platform already mentioned. This distinction of place, though censured in the passage just quoted from the Gospel, was reproduced in the Christian Church, where the bishop and his clergy occupied " chief seats " facing the congregation and with their backs to the altar. There was no separate gallery for women, but men sat together and women sat together within the one room.

Of officials in the Synagogue there were, in the New Testament period, only two of whom it is possible to feel sure. These were the Ruler of the Synagogue, and the person called the " minister " or " attendant " (Luke iv. 20). Neither of these held a position even remotely resembling that of a clergyman or minister in the Christian Church. The whole congregation were laymen (or women), there was no clerical order, still less a priestly one, and whatever was done in the course of the service was done by members of the congregation, and could be done (in theory) by any one of them.

The Ruler of the Synagogue was an elected president or chairman, or (if the term be allowed) managing director. He had the charge of the building, somewhat as trustee for the congregation, being responsible for its upkeep and maintenance, often probably at his own expense. In regard to the services, it was his duty to allot the different functions—such a one to recite the prayers, such others to read from the Torah and the prophets. He did not recite or read himself, unless there were on occasion a general desire that he should do so. Whenever the congregation met in the Synagogue, for worship or any other purpose, he was in charge of the meeting; and if anything occurred which called for notice or censure it was his duty to act as the occasion seemed to require. Thus (Luke xiii. 14) the Ruler of the Synagogue protested against the healing of the woman on the Sabbath. And (Acts xiii. 15) the Rulers of the Synagogue sent to Paul and Barnabas, inviting them to address the congregation. In the latter case the title is used in the plural, which probably only denotes the Elders, one of whom was, and any one of whom sooner or later might be, the acting " Ruler."

The other official who is certainly known to have functioned in the New Testament period is the "Hazan," a word for which there is no exact equivalent in English. His duty was mainly to act under the direction of the " Ruler," being caretaker of the building, attendant at the services, conveying the invitation of the " Ruler " to the various persons who were to take part, as above mentioned. He took the sacred scrolls out of the Ark, for the reading of the Scripture, and replaced them when the reading was over (see Luke iv. 17, 20). He was the executive officer who carried out any measure of discipline or punishment, *e.g.* scourging, that might be inflicted by the authorities of the Synagogue. He was probably a paid official, the only one in connexion with the Synagogue until long after the New Testament period. He did not himself take part in the service—the prayers and the reading—unless, presumably, there were on occasion a general desire that he should do so. On that occasion he would officiate just as an ordinary member of the congregation.

The service included reading from the Torah (and the prophets), prayer both public and private, the delivery of a discourse if there were any one present who was competent for such a task, and probably some singing, of selected Psalms. This is not absolutely certain ; but of course the singing of Psalms in the Temple was a long-established custom, and Matt. xxvi. 30 shows that devotional singing was familiar in a private company. As hymn-singing was a feature of Christian worship in very early times, it is reasonable to suppose that in this respect also the practice of the Church in congregational worship followed the example of the Synagogue.

The reading of the Torah was possibly the original root from which the whole institution of the Synagogue grew up, and it dated from a time before the canon of the prophetical books was finally closed. In the New Testament period, both Torah and Prophets were read, but it is not known how much, if indeed any, of the minute regulations observed in later times was in force then. What is certain is that those who " stood up to read " did so because they were invited to discharge that task. It is likely that, as in later times, a priest and a levite, if there happened to be any such present, would be called on to read before the ordinary layman. The passages read were usually very short, sometimes only two or three verses, probably with the intention of serving as the subject-matter for exposition. Thus Jesus, in the Synagogue at Nazareth (Luke iv. 17), read only two and a half verses from Isa. lxi., and proceeded to discourse about them. Presumably, a passage from the Torah had been previously read. In times later than the New Testament period, it became the custom to read the Torah through either in three years (Palestine) or in one year (Babylonia) ; the latter is the modern practice. But what was done, in this respect, in the New Testament period is not known ; and in any case no conclusion can be drawn from the later cycle as to what particular passage was read in the time of Jesus on a given date.

The prayers were recited, not read, and, in comparison with the length and complexity of the medieval liturgy, were few and simple. The two most ancient portions were: (1) the group of verses associated with the text " Hear, O Israel, the Lord our God is one Lord " (Deut. vi. 4–9, xi. 13–21 ; Num. xv. 37–41), called from its first word

"Shema" (hear). (2) The group of prayers usually called the Eighteen Benedictions. This was also called The Prayer, "tephillah," as if originally there had been hardly anything else in the service. It was also called "Amidah" (standing), because the worshippers stood while it was being recited. Both (1) and (2) are in use at the present day, though the form and contents of the latter have undergone much variation. Both must have been in use in the New Testament period. The oldest portions of (2) go back at least as far as the Maccabean time, and the series of eighteen is known to have been edited under the direction of Gamaliel II, in or about the year A.D. 80. It is therefore practically certain that they were in use, in some recognisable form, in the time of Jesus, so that he would join in them when he went to the Synagogue " as his custom was."

The prayers were recited by some member of the congregation called upon to do so by the Ruler of the Synagogue. The person who thus officiated was called the deputy or representative of the congregation (*sheliah ha-zibbur*) ; but he was so called for the particular occasion only. The title denoted not a fixed office, but an occasional function. It was his duty to "lead the congregation in prayer," to act with them and for them but not instead of them. The Synagogue has never recognised any one as having such power as that of a priest who administers a sacrament in the Christian Church. Judaism has no sacraments, and in that sense no priests. The leader or reciter of the prayers did not originally speak from the platform or the desk, if there was a desk; he simply stood up wherever he happened to be in the Synagogue. It may have been so in the time of Jesus; but the obvious convenience of the practice of reading or reciting from one place so as to be heard by all must have soon made itself felt. The phrase " to go before the Ark," meaning to recite the Eighteen Benedictions, can be traced to the first century A.D., and may be older.

The prayers thus recited were intended to express the thoughts and feelings of a worshipping congregation; and responses, one of which was the " Amen," familiar in Christian use, enabled the worshippers to take a real part in the service. There was also some opportunity for private prayer, during the time of worship.

The recital of the " Shema " and of the Eighteen Benedictions is the only part of the liturgy of which it is reasonably certain that it existed in the New Testament period substantially the same as it is found in later times. Yet in actual amount it is so small that we are almost obliged to conclude that other prayers were offered or passages read or sung; but of any such additional matter nothing is known.

There remains to be considered the discourse or sermon. This was, from the nature of the case, only included in the service if there were any one present who was able to speak with knowledge and acceptance. There was not, until quite modern times, any regular preacher at any given Synagogue. The Synagogue discourse is one of the sources from which the Christian sermon is derived; to this extent at least the Jewish practice passed into

Christian use. The form, however, changed considerably; and in the Synagogue the discourse was always an exposition of Torah with a view to edification. The contents of the haggadic midrashim (see above, p. 56 fol.) are probably for the most part the remains of Synagogue discourses. If a " doctor of the law " or other learned man happened to be present, he would naturally be invited to give an address, at the close of the prayers; but the case of Paul and Barnabas (Acts xiii. 16) goes to show that even strangers were invited to speak. The Synagogue never imposed a doctrinal test on its members, and thus could hear conflicting opinions, content to judge each on its merits. It is worth notice that Jesus continued to " teach in the Synagogues," which means to give the discourse in the service, when he was already known; and it does not appear that he was ever forbidden to do so. Moreover, during the last week of his life he " sat daily in the Temple teaching " (Mark xiv. 49), which amounts to much the same thing, so far as public speech is concerned.

It became the practice in later times for the preacher to address his discourse not directly to the congregation but in a low voice to an assistant, who repeated it aloud, more or less in his own words. But this practice, if known, was not general in the New Testament period; and the two cases just mentioned, of Jesus in the Synagogue at Nazareth and Paul in that at Antioch of Pisidia, seem to allow no room for anything of the kind.

The service, of which a general description has been here given, was no doubt varied according as it was held in the morning, afternoon or evening, on a Sabbath or a week-day, or on one or other of the festivals; but the two characteristics of un-adorned simplicity and of democratic organisation were never abandoned, and have not been down to the present day, even though the liturgy has become very long and elaborate.

It has been stated already that the Synagogue was never exclusively a place of worship; and this is true, though it is possible that where the building contained several rooms, as can be seen in some of the ruined Synagogues of Galilee, the room or hall where services were held was not used for other purposes. But it is stated, *e.g.*, that the punish-ment of scourging was inflicted in the Synagogue; and there is reason to believe that this was done outside or in one of the smaller rooms. If, for want of such, it were done in the actual place of meeting, it would be done at a time when service was not going on. It seems reasonable to suppose that the tribunal, *beth din*, by whose orders alone such punishment could be inflicted, held its session in one of the rooms of the Synagogue, or in the meeting-room itself, as being the most convenient or the only available place. More will be said about this when we come to consider the relation of the first Christians to the Synagogue, in the light of such texts as " in their Synagogues they will scourge you " (Matt. x. 17).

There remain a few references to Synagogues which call for brief notice. While it was scarcely possible for a small town or village to have more than one Synagogue, an important city might have several, and these distinguished by name as the meeting-houses of particular groups of people having some special reason for associating together. Thus, in Acts vi. 9, it is said, " there arose certain of them that were of the synagogue called (the synagogue) of the Libertines, and of the Cyrenians, and of the Alexandrians and of them of Cilicia and Asia." These were all Synagogues in Jerusalem, provided by and intended for the use of the various groups of persons named. The " Libertines " were such as had been slaves and had obtained their freedom. The others were foreign residents who liked to have their own meeting-house in Jerusalem, much as the French, Germans, Dutch, etc., have their own churches in London, Paris and elsewhere. In the cities of the Diaspora (the dispersion, Jewish centres of population outside Palestine), the same distinction of Synagogues is found. In Rome there was even a Synagogue of the Hebrew-speaking Jews as distinguished from those who spoke the vernacular—Latin, or possibly Greek. A Synagogue was sometimes called by the name of some principal benefactor, or even by the name of the emperor. Nothing is known in detail of the special characteristics of these Synagogues. It would seem probable that the general type of service was much the same in all, since the Synagogue as such was or had come to be a Pharisaic institution, while yet there would be slight differences of usage in the form of the prayers, etc. The same concern for the ancestral religion which led to the founding of Synagogues in foreign lands where Jews lived would guard against any serious departure from the traditional teaching and practice. And this is shown by the fact that Paul, when he addressed the congregation in various of the Synagogues in the lands to which he journeyed, met with strong opposition from those Jews who were not prepared to accept his interpretation of the Scriptures, or his doctrine of the crucified Messiah. The congregations in some of these Diaspora Synagogues are described as both Jews and Greeks. Thus, at Iconium (Acts xiv. 1) we read of " a multitude of Jews and Greeks " who evidently attended the Synagogue. And in Acts xviii. 8 the Ruler of the Synagogue in Corinth is called Crispus, and in ver. 17 another is mentioned called Sosthenes, which names are certainly not Jewish in form, though it is possible that the men who bore them used them for intercourse with Gentiles and had strictly Jewish names for use within the community of Israel. Those who are referred to as Greeks were probably proselytes (converts) and " fearers of God " (see above, p. 75), because, otherwise, they would not have been present in the Synagogues. These would naturally be less inclined to oppose Paul than the born and bred Jews. And the presence of such, in considerable numbers, goes to show why Paul always began with the Synagogue when he visited some town for the first time in his journeys.

In accordance with the order indicated at the opening of this chapter, having dealt with the Temple and the Synagogue, we have now to speak of Judaism in operation in the ordinary life of the Jew. The line of treatment followed in regard to

the Temple and the Synagogue is hardly adapted
to a description of the ordinary life of the Jew,
because in the former case Judaism was focussed
in two definite institutions, of which each had its
own character and its own sphere of influence.
Judaism naturally had a great deal to do with deter-
mining the general life of the Jew, but it was spread
out over a countless number of actions, manners, and
customs, and might be said to vary from one individual to another. A detailed description would
need a volume all to itself, and will not be attempted
here. It will serve a more useful purpose if we
consider the general way in which Judaism was
brought to bear upon the life of the Jew, especially
in the period with which we are concerned.

There were many things which a Jew did and
which a Gentile would not do, also things from
which the Jew refrained while to the Gentile they
were matters of indifference. The observance of
the Sabbath was very general amongst Jews. The
degree of strictness varied, no doubt, between wide
limits; but a total disregard of the Sabbath would
probably end in the abandonment of Judaism altogether. The Sabbath is clearly a case in which
the Judaism of a Jew made itself very strongly
felt. The rite of circumcision is another. So also,
a Jew observed certain regulations in regard to his
food, as, *e.g.*, to refrain from eating pork, or meat
from an animal that had not been killed in a particular way, also at certain times to refrain from
eating leavened bread. A Jew might, and no
doubt did on occasion, neglect these and similar
observances; but he could not feel towards them

and the neglect of them the indifference which a Gentile would feel, supposing the Gentile knew anything about them. We read (Mark vii. 3) that " the Pharisees and all the Jews, except they wash their hands diligently, eat not, holding the tradition of the elders ; and when they come from the market-place, except they wash themselves, they eat not ; and many other things there be which they have received to hold, washings of cups and pots and brasen vessels." That may be true of the Pharisees, but it is not true in detail of " all the Jews," at all events in our period. Yet it shows one kind of way in which Judaism influenced the daily life of the ordinary Jew. The Gentile would not act so from any sense of obligation, if he did such things at all. In like manner, in regard to many actions in well-nigh every department of life ; the Jew acted in a particular way, or he refrained from doing this and that, for reasons which were in some way connected with his Judaism.

Now it has been explained above (see p. 54 fol.) that the Halachah was intended by the Pharisees as the rule of right conduct, the guide to the exactly right way of fulfilling such and such a precept given in the Torah. And, as the determination of Halachah was in a very real sense the laying down of the law, the conclusion is drawn that the Pharisees imposed heavy burdens upon those who followed their teaching ; and that whereas before the Pharisees began to elaborate the Halachah life had been a comparatively simple matter, they made it difficult, complicated and for some people intolerable, so that they broke away from it, or refused to take the yoke of such obedience upon them. Whatever small amount of truth there may be in this statement, it does not take account of all the factors in the case, nor represent them correctly. And one factor thus omitted is the part played by use and custom in shaping the course of Jewish life. While it is perfectly true that the Pharisees refined the Halachah into minute detail, upon a great variety of subjects, they did not invent the subjects themselves. The observance of the Sabbath, the practice of circumcision, the distinction between allowed and forbidden food, between states of cleanness and uncleanness, were of immemorial antiquity. Some of them are enjoined in the Pentateuch, as express divine commands, others are mentioned there as customs. What their real origin was and when they began to be practised is mere matter of conjecture. They were at some time and in some way brought into association with religion, and their inclusion as definite precepts in the Torah is the proof that this was so, and the guarantee that it should continue to be so. The ancient custom, whatever it was, would endure not only because it was custom but also because it had some sanction of religion behind it; and what was done might be some simple act, performed but not much thought about, to be done because it was the proper thing to do and was in some way a religious observance.

Now the legislation contained in the Pentateuch was to some extent, and probably a very large extent, intended to bring these immemorial customs within the range of religion, meaning the religion of the priests and prophets under whose influence the books of the Pentateuch assumed the form in which they have come down. Possibly these customs had always had a religious significance; but, whether the Pentateuch was the work of Moses or the gradual accumulation of successive deposits of priestly or prophetic teaching, the religion which inspired it was of a higher order than that which had been in the ancient times before it. The ancient customs, usages, institutions were brought under the sanction of the higher teaching, or if they could not be so brought were disapproved or denounced. The point is that the legislator, or legislators, of the Pentateuch were not introducing novelties when they laid down laws which in form were new. They were dealing, in many cases at all events, with what was old, and very old at that, but were bringing it into an association with religion, their own religion, which it had not had till then. No doubt there were novelties. Festivals like Purim, connected with Esther and Mordecai, and that of Hanukkah, commemorating the triumph of the Maccabeans, obviously were not matters of immemorial usage. The rite of the water-drawing on the last day of the Feast of Tabernacles (referred to in John vii. 37) was of comparatively recent date in the New Testament period, being probably a creation of the Pharisees. But, even in such cases, it would be in accordance with the general course of Jewish history to suppose that the usage arose first and was then taken over and associated with religion.

Immemorial custom (for which the technical name in Hebrew is "*minhag*"), more or less con-

M

nected with religion, had a very great deal to do
with shaping the ordinary life of the Jew; and the
same is true in varying degree, no doubt, of every
people at some stage of its development. And it
is a usual experience that custom can endure merely
as custom, when such religious association as it
may have acquired is almost forgotten except in
name. Before the Exile there was sufficient of
the Pentateuchal legislation in existence to give
definite religious sanction to a great deal of ancient
custom; but that association was not strong enough
to make the religion effective in the life of the
people, and the national disaster of the Exile was
the result. Now we have seen (above, p. 32 fol.)
that the work of Ezra was first and foremost to
make the Torah the supreme authority in the
religious life of the Jewish people; and this means,
amongst other things, that the sanctification of
immemorial usage was definitely reasserted. The
old customs must be recognised to be religious
duties; and if they could not be so recognised they
must be given up. Old institutions might be
brought under new regulations, but it was for the
purpose of drawing closer the association with
religion, and of deepening the religious significance
of what had been inherited from earlier times.
And, unless it had been so, it is hard, if not impossible, to explain how, on the critical theory of
the gradual growth of the Pentateuch, the successive enlargements and modifications could have
been accepted. Beneath them all was the sub-
stratum of immemorial usage, gradually made to
express the ideas of a religion rising to loftier

spiritual heights. In that gradual ascent was the innovation.

With the Torah as Ezra left it, the life of the Jew was, potentially, a religious life in a sense in which it had not been before. If the Torah were really to be made the guide of life, then many actions of every-day occurrence would have a religious importance unfelt till then. And when this was recognised the need would be felt of some authoritative guidance to show what the Torah really enjoined and what was the right way of fulfilling its precepts. So we get, by another way, to the whole theory of the Torah and its interpretation worked out by the Pharisees, as explained in an earlier chapter. What was there said need not be here repeated. The point at present is this, that the Pharisees by means of the Halachah were attempting to solve the problem how to bring the life of the Jew, which was based on immemorial custom and which was now subjected to the immediate authority and control of the Torah, really and effectively within the range of religion; so that the Jew might feel that in doing the ordinary actions of his life, observing its ancestral usages, he was definitely and consciously serving God. The Halachah was no arbitrary enactment of new laws, unconnected with the past. It always stood in a close relation to the ancient custom ("minhag") upon any given subject; and the Halachah was never finally fixed until careful note had been taken of the custom. It occasionally happened that the custom was allowed to prevail, even though in theory the Halachah would enjoin a different

action, and from the example of such a case it is
easy to understand how the Pharisees and the later
Rabbis regarded the " minhag " (custom) as part
of the unwritten Torah, along with the Halachah.
It is needless to go into the minute details of the
subject.   What is of present importance is that the
real aim of the Pharisees was to bring the " minhag," the customary life of the Jew, more and more
completely into relation with religion, by showing
that it had a basis in the Torah or could be connected therewith.   The Halachah was the means
by which they did this ; and, in theory, the Halachah
was the " minhag " stated in terms of Torah.   In
practice it was not always possible to make that
re-statement, and the definition of Halachah was a
slow process, extending over centuries, far beyond
the New Testament period.   But in principle the
process began long before that period, with the
early Scribes who took up the work of Ezra ; and
the meaning of it, from first to last, is the attempt
to make the Torah really effective as the supreme
authority in life by working out a harmony between
the " minhag," the customary usages, and the
divine precepts contained in the Torah.   It was
with this end in view that the interpretation of the
Torah was begun and carried on without ceasing,
because without it, as has been shown above, the
mere letter of the Torah, the written text of the
Pentateuch, would have gradually lost all touch with
real life, and would have ceased to be effective as a
guide.   Therefore the Halachah was devised in
order to make the teaching of the Torah really
effective, and in framing the Halachah it was

obviously necessary to consider what the " min-hag," customary usage, was, so as to bring this not merely into connexion with the Torah, but where possible to bring it up to the level of the religion based on the Torah.   Interpretation was applied to the written text of the Torah for the same purpose, namely to make it harmonise with the religion based upon the Torah.   For the growing moral sense of the Pharisaic teachers recognised that the precepts of the Torah, if taken literally, would in some cases lead to results which were merely negatively or even actually harmful.   Thus the written law of " an eye for an eye and a tooth for a tooth " was at a very early stage replaced by the imposition of a money penalty, on the ground that the literal carrying out of the law would work injustice and useless suffering.   The development of the Hala-chah in the hands of the Pharisees was intended for the purpose of making the Torah practicable, by showing how its precepts really could be, and there-fore ought to be, put into actual practice.   The refinement of detail in applying the Halachah more and more minutely was the necessary working out of this process, carried perhaps in some cases to lengths required for logical completeness rather than for practical guidance.   The whole method may be thought to be mistaken, by those who do not accept the premises from which the framers of the Halachah started.   But, on those premises, the Pharisees were entirely justified in what they did, and to represent them as engaged in mere hair-splitting trivialities and in piling heavy burdens upon the people in consequence, is to misunderstand what they were about. As for the " heavy burdens," no one was obliged to submit to the Pharisaic discipline if he did not wish to do so ; and, as a matter of fact, the great majority of the Jewish people did not accept it to its full extent. But, when all is said and done, the Pharisees gave a very strong lead in the direction of practical application of religion to life, and their influence, through the Synagogues, was felt far beyond their own immediate ranks. They were revered by the mass of the people, as religious leaders and teachers, even when their discipline was not as a whole accepted.

Thus, finally, the immemorial customs played a large part in shaping the life of all Jews, whether Pharisees or not ; and so far as the influence of the Pharisees did not make itself felt, the customs remained as they had been, with only so much, or so little, of connexion with religion as they might already possess. Also, which is important, with so much the less protection against the disturbing influence of close contact with Gentile custom.

Thus Judaism showed itself in operation, in Temple, Synagogue and ordinary life, under different forms and in varying strength, as a principle working outwards from a centre. The centre was the religion of Torah in its most intense and concentrated form, which was Pharisaism ; and the circumference was where it lost all consciousness of its identity as Judaism, and became merged in the surrounding Gentile world.

CHAPTER VI

THE IMPACT OF CHRISTIANITY ON JUDAISM

In the foregoing chapters an account has been given of Judaism as it was, to the best of the present writer's belief, in the New Testament period. And, if the description given be correct, it might be held that the object of this book, as announced in its title " Judaism in the New Testament Period," had been attained. It would then be left to the reader to estimate, as well as he could, the effect upon Judaism so formulated of the new movement which began with Jesus. He might be able to forecast the manner in which the Judaism which he has learned in some degree to understand would react towards the new influence that was beginning to work. To leave the subject here, however, would be to lay a rather heavy burden on the reader (if he chose to assume it) and would indeed be hardly fair ; for the knowledge of the way in which Judaism reacted to the Christian movement is certainly necessary for the understanding of Judaism in the New Testament period. The previous chapters might be enough to show how Judaism would probably express itself under given conditions ; it will be the object of the present and the following chapter to show how in fact Judaism did meet the new movement. The New Testament period is obviously the period within which

Judaism had to deal with the problems presented by the rise of the Christian movement; and, while it is quite true, as remarked in the opening of this book (see above, p. 12), that Judaism was hardly affected in its own character by the impact of Christianity, it is also true that Judaism was involved in a controversy, faced with an opposition, met by new ideas and principles, all of which called for decisive action on the part of those who were the leaders and exponents of Jewish ideas and principles. The New Testament presents the controversy from the Christian side, and from that side alone; not indeed that the New Testament is primarily a controversial book, but that its own positive message could not be stated without frequent reference to the relations between Judaism and the founder of Christianity and his earliest followers. He himself was a Jew by birth and upbringing, and in many respects he did not cease to be Jewish in thought and action, while yet he came to hold a position in which there was sharp hostility towards him on the part of the leaders of Judaism; and, in the end, though not in his lifetime, the Christian Church, which owned him as its founder, separated itself completely from the Judaism with which it had at first been so closely associated. The process of gradual opposition and eventual separation is to be traced in the New Testament, not as a connected story but by frequent allusion to its various stages, and by expression of thoughts and feelings awakened by the controversy as it became more acute. While it is, of course, true that the various writings which make up the New Testament were composed in order to present the Christian message, from one or another point of view, it can hardly be denied that all those writings were produced in a period of controversy, that they owe much of their point to the need of maintaining a side against opponents, and that those opponents were held to be deserving of severe condemnation.

Judaism was accordingly thrown into a state of strain by the rise of Christianity, and it thus becomes necessary to study Judaism as it was while enduring that strain, if we are to understand what Judaism was in the New Testament period. We have therefore to consider the impact of Christianity upon Judaism, and its result in the final separation of the one from the other. To this object the present and the succeeding chapter will be devoted, and when this has been done, the purpose of the writer will have been accomplished. The whole process, from the first appearance of Jesus down to the final separation of Christianity from Judaism will be considered, and that from the Jewish point of view; the object being not to make any comparison between the respective merits of the two religions, but to show how the process appeared to those who engaged in it on the Jewish side.

Judaism, being such as has been described in the preceding chapters, was confronted by something new, first in the appearance of Jesus himself and later in the persons of his followers, especially Paul. A state of opposition was quickly set up, and it did not pass away. On what was that opposition based? Why did Judaism, being what it was, object to the views and principles represented by Jesus and his followers? How did those views and principles appear to those who met them as Jews, having such views and principles of their own as have been set forth in the earlier chapters of this book ? That is the question to the answering of which we must now proceed. And an answer is all the more necessary because the relations between Judaism and Christianity, in the period covered by the New Testament, have almost always been presented from the Christian side, if only because the knowledge necessary to present them from the Jewish side has seldom if ever been available; seldom indeed has it apparently been recognised that there was or even could be a Jewish side at all, let alone one which could be and was seriously maintained by men who were deeply convinced of the truth and right of what they defended.

The impact of Christianity upon Judaism is a phrase which only gradually acquired a distinct meaning. For, when Jesus began his ministry, he spoke as a Jew to Jews, and was regarded as such by those who heard him. What he said did not at the outset call forth any opposition, being apparently on Jewish lines familiar to all. We read (Mark i. 14) that " after John was delivered up Jesus came into Galilee, preaching the gospel of God, and saying, The time is fulfilled, and the kingdom of God is at hand; repent ye and believe in the gospel." And later in the same chapter (ver. 21 fol.) we read how " he went into the Synagogue on the Sabbath day, and taught." Also (ver. 32 fol.) how " he healed many that were sick of divers diseases." And (ver. 39) how " he went into their Synagogues throughout all Galilee, preaching and casting out devils." There is nothing here to suggest that Jesus or his countrymen regarded what he was doing as anything new, that is, anything which was contrary to the ordinary Jewish ideas. And this is borne out in a remarkable way if the teaching of Jesus, as recorded in the Synoptic Gospels, is compared with the summary of the Pharisaic teaching given above (see Chap. III, pp. 80–118). Such a comparison discloses the fact that there was a very considerable extent of common ground in the two bodies of teaching. Whatever may be the explanation of the presence of this common ground, the existence of it cannot be denied. That is to say, parallels can be found in the Rabbinical literature for perhaps as much as 90 per cent. of the recorded sayings of Jesus. Of course, opinions will be divided as to the worth of those parallels, and upon this question more will be said below ; but, so far as they go, they have to be reckoned with. They cannot be put on one side as of no value. This question of the common ground between the teaching of Jesus and the teaching of the Pharisees is of importance in answering the larger question why there was opposition towards him on their part. It will be therefore strictly relevant to the present purpose to go somewhat at length into this matter of the " common ground."

Jewish scholars have been at much trouble to show the likeness between the teaching of Jesus and that of the Pharisees, as contained in the Rabbinical literature ; and they have been able to prove beyond any question the existence of a close relationship between the two, extending over a wide range of subjects. Christian scholars have usually held that, while there is similarity in the form of words, Jesus put a more spiritual meaning on the words than the Pharisees did. It would be difficult if not impossible to prove an assertion of this kind; any argument to be of weight would have to be based on a thorough knowledge not only of what the Rabbinical teachers said but also of what they meant by it. And such knowledge is seldom found where it is most needed. Apart from such knowledge, to assert the superiority of the teaching of Jesus over that of the Pharisees, where they are alike in form, is merely to beg the question.

Much more important is the fact that no challenge was made from the one side or from the other in regard to the teaching which formed the " common ground." The Pharisees did not suggest that Jesus was teaching something new when he used the term " Our Father who is in heaven," in reference to God. Jesus did not put forward any claim that he was using that term in a higher and more spiritual sense than that in which the Pharisees used it. Alike on the one side and on the other it was simply taken for granted and used as being part of the then customary language of religion. The same is true of all the rest of the common ground. The absence of challenge or even of remark on either side is proof that the ground really was common to both; and it is a proof which quite outweighs any hazardous assertion of the superiority of one body of teaching over the other.

The fact of the existence of this common ground is not open to dispute; but to account for it is quite another matter. How did there come to be this large body of teaching common to both parties? Did the Pharisees borrow it all from Jesus, or did he borrow it all from them? And if neither borrowed from the other, what then? Jewish scholars very naturally have held that he got it all from the Pharisees, or at all events from the Jewish teachers of his time and earlier. Christian scholars have replied that the evidence on which the supposed borrowing is alleged to have taken place is all, or nearly all, of a date later than that of Jesus, so that he could not have been the borrower. There is truth in both these assertions, but they do not go the whole way towards solving the problem.

If it be meant, on the Jewish side, that Jesus learned the various doctrines which he taught from the lips of one or more of the leading Pharisaic teachers of his time, there is nothing to show that he ever had even the opportunity of hearing such a teacher. The story in Luke ii, about Jesus as a boy of twelve years of age sitting among the doctors in the Temple, is, as I have shown above (p. 147), not ruled out by anything in the known usages of the time. But, even if the story be admitted, the time spent by the boy Jesus in the manner described is hardly enough to allow of his learning so much of Pharisaic teaching as is found in what I have called the " common ground." Apart from that one incident—and I lay no stress on it—nothing is known of any intercourse that he may have had with any leading Pharisaic teacher, and nothing to make it in the least degree likely that he ever had such inter-course. To assert that he had or that he must have had such intercourse is again merely to beg the question. If there was any borrowing of the material which forms the common ground, it cannot be shown that Jesus was the borrower.

But neither did the Pharisees borrow from Jesus. The argument from the later date of the Rabbinical parallels to his teaching has already been partly answered (see above, p. 82 fol.). It was there shown that the late date is that of the compilation of the Midrash in which the relevant passages are found, while the contents of the Midrash are considerably earlier, and go back to a time well within the New Testament period. Moreover, there is no noticeable breach of continuity in the substance of the teaching contained in the Haggadah, which forms the basis of the comparison with the teaching of Jesus. If this argument be well founded, it proves that in spite of their apparently later date the Rabbinical parallels to the teaching of Jesus were not necessarily of later origin, let alone borrowed from him. Those who do not know the Rabbinical literature will perhaps be hardly convinced by this argument, and will continue to think that after all the Rabbis borrowed from Jesus the doctrines which form the common ground. A proof, however, can be given which should convince the strongest advocate of this view that however plausible it may appear it is nevertheless untenable. A story * is told in the Talmud of which it will be useful to translate a portion here.

---

* The passage, with its Talmudic references and commentary, will be found in my *Christianity in Talmud and Midrash*, pp. 137–145. To give direct references to Rabbinical passages would not be helpful to the readers for whom this book is mainly intended.

A very eminent Pharisee, Rabbi Eliezer ben Hor-
kenos, was once put on his trial on a charge of being
a Mīn, which in this connexion denotes a Christian.
He was greatly troubled in mind; and, although he
was acquitted, he could not get over the shame of
having incurred such a charge.   His disciples tried
to console him, but in vain.   Then one of them,
Rabbi Akiba, said to him (and here I translate):
" ' Rabbi, shall I say to thee why thou art perhaps
grieving ? '   He said to him, ' Say on.'   He said to
him, ' Perhaps one of the Minim (Christians) has
said to thee a word of Minuth (Christian teaching),
and it has pleased thee.'   He said to him, ' Akiba,
thou hast reminded me.   Once I was walking in the
upper street of Sepphoris, and I found a man, of the
disciples of Jeshu the Nazarene, and Jacob of
Chephar Sechanja was his name; and he said to
me, ' It is written in your Torah ' " [and then follows
a reference to Deut. xxiii. 19, " Thou shalt not bring
the hire of a harlot," etc., together with an interpretation of it prefaced by the words, ' Thus hath Jeshu
the Nazarene taught me.' "   Rabbi Eliezer went on]
" ' And the saying pleased me, and because of this
I was arrested for Minuth, and I transgressed what
is written in the Torah (Prov. v. 8), " Keep thy way
far from her," this is Minuth ; " and come not nigh
the door of her house," this is the Government.' "

The Rabbi Eliezer who appears in this story was
one of the chief Pharisaic teachers of his time.   He
died A.D. 117 or thereabouts, and he must have been
born not many years after the crucifixion of Jesus.
Now if he felt so strongly at the mere thought of
having anything to do with what came from Jesus

the Nazarene, it is quite inconceivable that the Pharisees should have adopted from Jesus all the mass of teaching which forms what I have called the " common ground," and should have made it their own while ignoring where it came from. And the reason is clear. If they borrowed it, that could only be because they had not got it already and therefore took it over as something new. In that case, they could not possibly be ignorant whence it came and from whom they had learned it. But the case of Rabbi Eliezer, in the story quoted above, shows that they would not, knowingly, take anything at all from that particular source. What may be called the official condemnation of Jesus by the Pharisees is the statement, " Jesus . . . practised magic and deceived and led astray Israel " (see *Christianity in Talmud and Midrash*, p. 83). Men who thought thus of Jesus would never dream of adopting as their own anything that he taught.

We may therefore rule out the suggestion that the body of doctrine forming the "common ground" was borrowed by either party from the other, and we must look elsewhere for the explanation. Nor need we look far. The most natural and obvious source for the common teaching is the Synagogue. The suggestion that Jesus arrived at the doctrines which he taught by his own independent study of the Scriptures, does not meet the point which has to be explained. It would be remarkable if Jesus and the Jewish teachers, on lines of study pursued quite independently of each other, arrived at results not merely similar but sometimes identical. The teaching which forms the " common ground " has

to be accounted for, and also the fact that it was
common, taught alike by Jesus and the Pharisees.
To assign the Synagogue as the source of it, is a
simple and natural explanation, and one that really
explains. It has been shown above (pp. 27, 161 fol.)
that the Synagogue was both a place of worship and
a place of teaching. The teaching given was interpretation of Torah on the lines of Haggadah, *i.e.*
for edification, covering the ground of theology and
ethics, and including certainly such subjects as those
which belong to the " common ground." The
summary of Pharisaic teaching given in Chapter
III is all based on teaching given in the Synagogue,
for the Synagogue was developed and maintained
entirely on Pharisaic lines, and the teaching given
there was in accordance with their ideas. When
therefore Jesus " entered as his custom was into the
Synagogue on the Sabbath day " (Luke iv. 16) he
would hear from week to week and from year to year,
as he lived and grew up in Nazareth, such teaching
as forms the " common ground," including (be it
noted) the frequent use of the parable as a form of
teaching. When he grew up to manhood and
came to be a teacher himself, he never raised any
objection to this teaching nor challenged it in any
way. If he had done so it would obviously be
excluded from the " common ground." He used
the parable form himself, and he never said a word
against the Synagogue as a religious institution.
It was not in regard to these subjects that he opposed
the Pharisees or that they denounced him. For
him and for them the teaching in question contained
just the current concepts of religion expressed in the

N

customary words and phrases. That Jesus was a man of profound spiritual power and daring originality needs not to be shown. But his originality showed itself elsewhere than in the teaching which was common to him and to the Pharisees, and his spiritual power was none the less great if he found adequate expression for his religious ideas in the same terms which they also used. After all, is it wonderful that a man who had grown up from boyhood under the constant influence of home and Synagogue, should instinctively use the religious language which was familiar to him by long association, and use it intentionally because he felt that it was true and expressed what he meant to say, although in other respects he diverged widely from the ways of his fathers and set at nought the Tradition of the Elders ?

The fact that there was this common ground between Jesus and the Pharisees, extending over so wide a range of subjects, does not of course prove that he himself was a Pharisee. It would be hardly necessary to make this remark, if it were not that some Jewish scholars have gone far towards the assertion that he was. Chwolson and, in the present time, Klausner, in his remarkable book *Jesus of Nazareth*, have stressed the likeness between Jesus and the Pharisees to such an extent that it is hard to see why there should ever have been any opposition between them, let alone such an antagonism as is presented in the Gospels. Whatever he was, Jesus was most certainly not a Pharisee. The " common ground " proves nothing in this respect. If two circles intersect there is an area common to both, but they are two circles and not one.   If they were identical, or if one were included in the other, they would not intersect.   So, Jesus and the Pharisees were very far indeed from being identical, while yet they shared some " common ground." If they had not had that " common ground " they could not have come into any relation or contact with each other.   The Pharisees had some, even a considerable amount, of common ground with the Zealots, some with the Sadducees, some with the Essenes and some even with the Am ha-aretz ; but yet the Pharisees were not Zealots, nor Sadducees, nor Essenes, nor Am ha-aretz, and were very definitely aware of the distinction in each case.   So Jesus, in spite of any common ground, was certainly not a Pharisee, certainly not a Sadducee, certainly not a Zealot and certainly not an Essene. So far as he can be classed under any of the terms then in current use, he was an Am ha-aretz.

To say that Jesus was an Am ha-aretz is indeed only another way of saying that he was not a Pharisee.   But, while the term itself has a wide range of meaning (see above, pp. 72–74), the application of it to Jesus throws a good deal of light both on the position he held as a religious and social worker and on the lines which he followed in his teaching ; and in this way it helps to a right understanding of the situation in which the opposition between him and the Pharisees was developed, the first impact of the Christian movement upon Judaism.   We read of Jesus (Mark vi. 34) that he " saw a great multitude, and he had compassion on them, because they were as sheep not having a shepherd; and he began to teach them many things." He preached in the Synagogues, as in Capernaum and Nazareth and many other places, but he also preached to the people in village and countryside wherever he chanced to find them. Of his recorded words comparatively few are said to have been addressed to the congregation in a Synagogue, and the words so spoken either were or became the occasion of controversy. By far the greater number of his recorded words are said to have been spoken out of doors—by the lake, on the hillside, in the open field or the village street.

Now the direct influence of the Pharisees as religious teachers was exerted chiefly, though perhaps not entirely, through and in the Synagogues. There they taught, or provided teaching for, those who attended the Synagogue. But they did not make any special point of trying to get hold of the people outside, so as to teach and enlighten them. Consequently there were many who were without any religious teaching, being (for whatever reason) not attendants at any Synagogue, yet willing to respond to such teaching if it were offered to them and brought to them. These are the "sheep without a shepherd," and these are they to whom Jesus especially ministered. To do so outside the Synagogue was something new. John the Baptist, it is true, did not preach in the Synagogues; but he remained in the desert or by the Jordan, and people went to hear him or not as they chose. Jesus went about amongst the people, in the places where they lived, and no one before him had ever done so. He went to them as one of themselves, with a

sympathy such as no teacher had ever shown to
them.   And he gave to them the teaching which is
to be read in the Gospels—the Sermon on the
Mount, the Lord's Prayer, many of the Parables,
besides many other great sayings.   These were
addressed by him to his friends, whether the multitude to whom he felt drawn or the smaller group
who had gathered round him as his disciples and
chosen companions.   And while the teaching for the
most part was not in itself new, being on the lines
of current teaching in the Synagogue, to most of his
hearers it would be new ; and he himself uttered it
not because it was what was taught in the Synagogue
but because it was what he meant to say—none the
worse for being hallowed by old association.   Speaking thus to the few or the many, his chosen disciples
or the multitude, he spoke with the freedom born of
mutual trust and sympathy, not needing to fear
either suspicion or hostility.   Indeed, at the outset
of his career there is nothing to show that his
teaching awakened either suspicion or hostility.   It
is Jesus, as he thus opened his heart to his friends,
who has won the hearts of all in all ages since who
have learned from him by reading his words in the
Gospels.   There is no need, in this connexion,
critically to sift his recorded sayings and to distinguish between those which he did and those which
perhaps he did not utter.   The general fact stands
fast that he did speak to the people under some
such conditions, and in some such way, and with
some such thoughts and feelings, as those just
indicated.

Now, whatever occasion of controversy might

arise between himself and the Pharisees, as his public ministry became more widely known, it was not connected with such teaching as is here in question—that, namely, which formed the "common ground." Moreover, in this public teaching he was not always, or perhaps often, thinking about the Pharisees at all; certainly not in his earlier addresses to the multitudes. He had as little to do with the Pharisees as his hearers had, they and he being alike Am ha-aretz together. He was not out to bid them all come to Synagogue, he was there to say just what he wanted to say, and he said it, without keeping a careful eye on the Synagogue all the time. Some of his teaching was not on the lines of that given in the Synagogue, and he gave it simply because it was what he meant and believed, and not with any special reference to the Synagogue or the Pharisees whose ideas the Synagogue expressed. This is part, though it is only a part, of what is meant when it is said (Mark i. 22) that he "taught them as having authority and not as the Scribes." And, in the well-known series of comparisons in Matt. v. : "Ye have heard that it was said . . . but I say unto you . . ." there is, if I am right, no special reference to the Pharisees or what they taught in the Synagogue. The reference is simply to notions which his hearers might have in their minds, notions picked up from anywhere according to chance and opportunity. One of these comparisons is (Matt. v. 43), "Ye have heard that it was said, Thou shalt love thy neighbour and hate thine enemy, but I say unto you," etc. Every one knows that nowhere in the Old Testament is there a command " Thou shalt hate thine enemy " ; and it is equally true, though not every one knows it, that there is no such command in the Rabbinical, *i.e.* Pharisaical, literature.   To say that Jesus had the Pharisees in mind when he uttered the words in question is to attribute to him a pointless and irrelevant remark.   But it is quite another matter if he were referring merely to some popular notion which his hearers might have got hold of, something which he or they had heard in common talk, some scrap of what might pass for religious teaching, and which would supply a sharp contrast to the teaching which he wished to give.   He was out to give them the good and the true, and not merely to criticise what others had said.   Who the others might have been did not matter, so long as he could use what they said as a means of driving home his own lesson.   This seems a more natural explanation than to assume, as some have done, that " Ye have heard " represents a technical term of debate in the Rabbinical schools.   Such a term would be quite unintelligible both to Jesus and to his hearers, and it is not probable that he had ever heard it.

If what has been advanced above be true, then in most of his recorded teaching (apart from controversy), and especially that addressed to his disciples or to the multitude, Jesus was not thinking of the Pharisees any more than his hearers were, and he opened his heart to his friends and showed to them that side of his nature which has held the reverent love and wonder of his followers ever since.   Now this side of his character the Pharisees never beheld, and never had any chance of beholding.   Simply because, as his ministry developed and he and they met more and more frequently, their presence necessarily put an end to the feeling of mutual trust and affection which had pervaded all his intercourse with his friends. The Pharisees brought in the note of suspicion and challenge which till then had been absent. As has been stated, there were comparatively few Pharisees in Galilee at that time, and no eminent teacher. They came in, attracted no doubt by the fame of Jesus, to see and hear for themselves what was going on. And they very soon observed that he and his disciples did not "walk according to the Tradition of the Elders." They made no remark about his teaching, which was mostly what they were accustomed to in the Synagogues. But his practice was not at all in accordance with their ideas. So they challenged him, or his disciples, and that more than once. "Why doth your master eat with publicans and sinners?" (Matt. ix. 11); "Behold, thy disciples do that which it is not lawful to do on the Sabbath" (Matt. xii. 2); "Why do thy disciples transgress the tradition of the elders?" (Matt. xv. 2). And on each occasion they were answered with a sharp retort. Which is no doubt perfectly natural, but it shows how far Jesus and the Pharisees stood aloof from each other, never having till then come into close contact with one another. He spoke to the multitude as to his friends; he spoke to the Pharisees as to suspicious critics who might, and who in fact very soon did, become active opponents. Each was seen by the other in the least favourable aspect. The Pharisees never saw him, and never could see him, as his friends of the multitude saw him. And he never saw the Pharisees with any sympathetic discernment of what they really meant by their religion. He saw, as an outsider could only see, what they did; and, like any outsider, he had no clue to understand why they did it. To him they were the representatives of hidebound pedantry, enemies to all the working of the free spirit. To them he was a dangerous revolutionary, threatening to undermine the very foundations of their religious system. If the comparison may be allowed, the Pharisees and Jesus regarded each other in a way somewhat like that in which Conservatives would regard an extreme Labour leader, and *vice versa* (of course, without any political implication). It is beside the mark to say that they ought to have owned the beauty and truth of his teaching, and have given way before the superiority of one such as Christian eyes have seen him. They had no quarrel with his teaching, which to a large extent was the same as their own Haggadah. They did not see that side of him which his disciples saw. They only saw the man who was making light of, and even rejecting, that without which religion was to them inconceivable. It is usual to assume that Jesus must have known all about all the Judaism of his time, in all its several phases. As a matter of fact, the only part that he did know intimately was the life, thought, religion and morality of the Am ha-aretz class to which he belonged.

But this is to anticipate the discussion of the real cause of opposition between Jesus and the Pharisees; and before that can be dealt with there are certain other topics which must be touched on. So far, we have reached the conclusion that the opposition was not based on his teaching, since so much of it was what the Pharisees also taught. It is true that on some points they challenged his teaching, as *e.g.* in regard to whether a man could forgive sins (see above, p. 103); which only serves to show how in other respects they mainly agreed with him, apart from the real ground of opposition to be dealt with presently. So far as the teaching is concerned which forms the " common ground," and which includes by far the larger part of what is recorded in the Synoptic Gospels, it is obvious that it was not on this side of his ministry that the originality of Jesus lay. When people say, How beautiful, how wonderful, how deep yet simple is the teaching of Jesus, they say what is abundantly true; but that which they thus praise is almost entirely Jewish and not peculiar to Jesus. When he is referred to as a teacher, or as *the* Teacher, or the Great Teacher, the emphasis is wrongly placed. He was a teacher, no doubt; but in most of what he taught he was not original, since he gave for the most part what was only the current teaching of the Synagogue. And in regard to what was not part of the common ground, the amount of it, apart from the special matter of controversy, was small and not enough by itself to account for his greatness. The Christian Church when it came into being took over his teaching not on its own merits, but because it was his; and being his, it was in form and substance almost entirely Jewish. In this new setting, the old words and ideas which had been known before his time in the teaching of the Synagogue shone out as never before, but only to reveal the truth, beauty and depth which had been in them all along, as much when they had been imparted by Pharisees as when they were uttered by Jesus. It was not as Teacher that Jesus laid hold of mankind to the extent that he has done, and it was not as Teacher that he was first proclaimed to the Gentile world by the earliest messengers of the gospel. The central thought of that earliest message was not the Teacher from Nazareth, but Christ crucified and risen from the dead, a Christ in whom the function of teacher was entirely lost sight of.

The foregoing discussion of the teaching of Jesus and the common ground which he shared with the Pharisees has not disclosed the real ground of opposition between him and them. But it has shown that the first impact of Christianity (in the person of its founder) upon the Judaism of his time was at that point, or on that broad front, denoted by Pharisaism. This was only natural, because the Pharisees were the only ones who would be likely to notice anything peculiar in what he was doing. He grew up in a village, as one of the people, born and bred in Judaism ; so that he could not be said to make any contact with Judaism as if it were something external to him. But an impact of the principles and ideas which he represented upon those for which Judaism stood was possible and did in fact come to pass. And, because the Pharisees were in close touch with the Synagogues, and because the Synagogues were to a large extent, though not exclusively, the scene of his ministry, it was the Pharisees first, and their "Scribes and doctors of the law," who came to learn more of what was going on and who this new teacher really was whose fame was beginning to spread through all Galilee : it was these with whom he first came into collision.

The Pharisees are the only ones with whom Jesus came into conflict until the very last days in Jerusalem, when he encountered the Sadducees in the person of the High Priest and his associates. With Essenes he had nothing to do. The Zealots, indeed, might have had a good deal to say to him if he had made any overtures to them; but he did not come into conflict with them, nor apparently take much notice of them. Yet it is worth observing that he had two Zealots in his chosen band of the Twelve, and that it was a Zealot who betrayed him. We have then to consider what there was in his teaching or his actions which would bring him into conflict with the Pharisees.

If there had been nothing else, it is safe to say that the fame of his works of healing, and of other wonders ascribed to him in popular report, would not of itself have set the Pharisees against him. They had already their ground of condemnation before they disparaged him for these things, by saying (Mark iii. 22), " He hath Beelzebub, and by the prince of the devils casteth he out the devils." It was not to the works of healing and the like merely as such that they objected; it was that by these acts a man, whom on other grounds they disliked and feared, acquired a dangerous influence over the minds of the people whereby he could

lead them astray. The works of healing and the
doing of wonders (whether real or reported) afford
no reason for the breach between Jesus and the
Pharisees. Neither does the supposed claim that
he was the Messiah ; for, whether he ever made
that claim or not, it would be the Sadducees far
more than the Pharisees who would be opposed to
it. The discussion of this Messianic claim will
therefore be reserved till we come to the opposition
between Jesus and the Sadducees, the second impact
of Christianity, in the person of Jesus, upon the
Judaism of his time.

What then really was the ground of opposition
between Jesus and the Pharisees ? In a sentence
it was this :—he repudiated the whole system of
the Halachah ; and he criticised, and on occasion
rejected, the Torah upon which the Halachah was
based. What has been said at length in an earlier
chapter of this book (see above, pp. 54–56) upon
the meaning of Halachah need not be repeated
here ; but unless the reader has realised the vital
importance of the Halachah in the Pharisaic system
of religion, he will not understand why the repudiation of it by Jesus should have been felt as a deadly
blow to religion as the Pharisees conceived it ; a
blow to be warded off if possible, in any case a
new and serious danger which would work untold
harm if it continued unchecked.

Several instances are given in the Gospels of
controversy between Jesus and the Pharisees on
questions of Halachah. Thus (Mark ii. 23 fol.)
there is the case of the disciples plucking the ears
of corn on the Sabbath ; (Mark iii. 1 fol.) the healing

on the Sabbath of a man who had a withered arm;
(Mark vii. 1 fol.) the eating with unwashed hands,
thereby transgressing the Tradition of the Elders,
i.e. the Halachah; (Mark vii. 9 fol.) the case of
Corban; (Mark x. 2 fol.) the question of divorce;
(Mark xii. 13 fol.) the question of giving tribute to
Cæsar. The long series of woes in Matt. xxiii. is
not an instance of controversy, but (so far as it is
authentic) a sort of final denunciation of his opponents after many controversies. As it stands now
it may well have been enlarged and sharpened by
the writer of the Gospel, in a time later than that of
Jesus when the hostility of the Christian Church
against Judaism had become acute. But, unless
there had been some foundation for it in what
Jesus actually said, it could hardly have been
ascribed to him. In itself, and considering that
Jesus at the time he is said to have uttered it was
in the position of a man fighting with his back to
the wall, it seems to the present writer entirely
likely that he should have uttered practically the
whole of it, except vv. 34–39, which are obviously
later than his time.

In regard to the various cases of controversy
enumerated above, one or two points should be
noted if the situation disclosed in them is to be
really understood. The question which of the two
parties was right in each case is not worth asking,
because each was right from his own point of view
and on his own principles. But the principles on
the two sides were fundamentally irreconcilable;
and, while both parties took their stand on the
doing of the will of God as the supreme duty, the

one, viz. the Pharisees, maintained the Halachah as the defined way of doing the divine will, based on the Torah, which was God's own revelation of his will, the other, viz. Jesus, maintained the individual conscience as the only guide to the right doing of the divine will. The opposition was irreconcilable because there was conscience on both sides, not on one only. The Halachah was worked out as an attempt to read the Torah by the light of the moral discernment of the teachers who defined it, from age to age. It never was, at any time, a mere cast-iron legislation. It always had its base in ethical discernment; and the difference between the Halachah and what might be called the free conscience is that the one is worked out in terms of an Idea, viz. Torah, and the other in terms of a Person, whether that Person were Jesus or any one of his followers. Therein, indeed, lies the deepest root of the fundamental difference between Judaism and Christianity; a difference which nothing can ever obliterate.

Now the Pharisees in their controversies with Jesus were concerned with the fundamental principle more than with the particular occasion of dispute; the arguments of Jesus were directed to the particular case. The two parties therefore did not exactly meet, or stand on the same plane. Neither clearly understood the position of the other, and apparently neither made the slightest attempt to do so. The collision came about through the alarm of the Pharisees at the actions of Jesus which were not in accordance with the Tradition of the Elders. Their uneasy questions were met either by a defence of the act objected to, as in the case of the plucking of corn on the Sabbath, or by a sharp retort, as in the case of Corban. There was no attempt at mutual explanation or understanding; at least none such is recorded or even hinted at, though there was abundant occasion for it. What is recorded shows clearly that Jesus had no close acquaintance with the Halachah which he denounced, and none at all with the theory of it. He had no opportunity, apparently, of acquiring such knowledge, for in Galilee, as already stated, there was in his time no halachic teacher so far as is known. If he had such knowledge, he would not have used the case of Corban as a weapon, for the case on that subject was quite other than he supposed; and, if he had had such knowledge, he would have understood that there was another side to the actions of the Pharisees beyond that which was offered to the gaze of the onlooker. They, on their side, could have learned much if they had tried to understand what Jesus really meant; but they were not encouraged to do so by the manner in which their objections and criticisms were received. If Jesus meant to make war on their system, *i.e.* on religion as they understood it, so be it, they would defend what to them was sacred, the divine revelation in the only form under which they had learned to recognise it. This is only what has been seen over and over again in history, when a prophet or reformer has denounced some system which he deemed corrupt or false; and there would be no reason to expect anything different in the case of Jesus and the Pharisees if it were not that his

own words about " Love your enemies," and of his
having been sent to save sinners, open the eyes of
the blind, lead back the lost, etc., might suggest
that the Pharisees, if they were all that he thought
them, were in especial need of such spiritual help
and healing as he could give.   The worse they
were, and the more hardened in their evil ways,
the more remarkable is the total absence of any
attempt on his part to bring them to a better frame
of mind.   The " lost sheep of the house of Israel,"
to whom alone he said he was sent, apparently did
not include the Pharisees, though as he saw them
they were in worse case than any of the Am ha-aretz.
It is not wonderful that the Pharisees should regard
him, as they certainly did, as a dangerous enemy ;
and, though they had no part in bringing about his
death, they might well feel that it put an end to a
great danger to religion, as they understood it.

What has been said above represents, in the view
of the present writer, the meaning of the controversy
with Jesus as it appeared from the Jewish and more
particularly the Pharisaic side.   There is the more
reason for so presenting it because the Christian
reader of the Gospels has usually no means of
knowing how the case looked from the Jewish side,
and seldom any idea that there was a Jewish side,
except in the sense that the opposite of white is
black.

The impact of Christianity on Judaism was thus
made on that side represented by the Pharisees, and
it took the form of a repudiation of the Halachah
and the assertion of liberty to criticise even the
Torah itself.   The opposition thus declared was

o

never withdrawn on the one side or on the other; but it may be doubted if it would have led to any serious consequence, let alone to the death of Jesus, unless other and quite different causes provoked hostility from other representatives of Judaism. So far as the Pharisees were concerned, it does not appear that they took any particular measures to silence Jesus; we do not hear that he was excommunicated, or even that the Synagogues were closed against him. Beyond severe disapproval of him there was not much that they could do; and if Jesus after a time left Galilee, finding that he could make no impression on its people, and went up to Jerusalem, that was at least as much his own act as the result of any expulsion by the Pharisees. Even the Gospels do not represent him as having been driven out.

The resolve to go to Jerusalem and seek a hearing there led to the second phase of the impact on Judaism, because he there came into conflict with the Sadducees, not so much in their capacity as Sadducees but as the party enjoying the prestige of the Temple and vitally interested in the maintenance of the whole official system of which the Temple was the seat. Presumably, if he had not gone to Jerusalem he would not have become involved in that controversy which proved fatal to him. At least, during his Galilean ministry he said little or nothing about the Temple or the abuses which sheltered within its courts. Even in Jerusalem his attack on the Temple seems to have been mainly confined to the incident of the cleansing of the Temple; but while the battle of the closing days was fought over other ground, and brought in the question whether he claimed to be the Messiah or not, it was nevertheless a sure instinct of self-defence, on the part of the Sadducees and all who were concerned with the vested interests of the priesthood, to bring about his death. They used the Messiah question as a means of making Jesus out to be a political offender, and thereby of procuring his execution by the Roman governor. Without the permission of the governor they could not have put Jesus to death, and they would have had no case if he were accused before Pilate on merely religious grounds. The claim to be the Messiah, even if Jesus had made such a claim and made it openly, was not in itself a religious offence, and could not have been condemned and punished by any Jewish tribunal, so to speak, on its own merits. But it had a political side, and that side was turned and used against Jesus, not because it was justified, but because it would serve the purpose of those who sought to destroy him. It will therefore be necessary to consider the question of the Messiahship in reference to Jesus, a question on which an immense amount has been written and which has as yet received no answer accepted as final. Perhaps a final answer will never be reached, but yet something can be said, at all events from the Jewish side, which may be worth considering.

That Jesus throughout his whole career was in deadly earnest about something goes without saying. From the beginning to the end he preached a gospel, and the keynote of his preaching was the kingdom of Heaven, and the need of immediate preparation for it. What he said about it can be read in his recorded words and is well known to every reader of the Gospels. What was generally understood by the kingdom of Heaven has been explained above (see pp. 106–112); it was a purely Jewish conception, but had various aspects, of which now one and now another was emphasised. It began with the individual, as the rule of God in the heart; it easily passed into a collective form as of a state of society; it could acquire a political meaning in which it tended to become revolutionary; and it was, not invariably but commonly, associated with the expectation of the Messiah who should establish it and in the name of God rule over it. Now, whatever he meant by it, Jesus was concerned before everything else to preach the kingdom of God; for that he lived and worked, and for that in the end he died, in other words for the sake of what to him was of supreme importance. So much stands fast beyond any possibility of question.

Now the kingdom of God is one of the leading ideas in the Apocalyptic literature (see above, pp. 125–130), and in connexion with the kingdom a good deal is said in that literature about the Messiah. If therefore Jesus preached the kingdom of God, whatever he meant by it, the mere fact of his doing so would inevitably arouse attention to him in the minds of those in whom such ideas and expectations were present, notably among the Zealots, though more or less amongst the people generally, quite apart from any exact knowledge of Apocalyptic writings. It is probably impossible to determine exactly what Jesus had in his mind when he spoke of the kingdom of God, seeing that the term, as already explained, had several meanings and may have had more. It is even more difficult to determine what Jesus had in his mind as to his own position in reference to the kingdom which he proclaimed. If there were any decisive answer to be found in the available evidence, the question would not need to be so hotly debated as it has been and continues to be. The real solution of the problem died with Jesus himself. He undoubtedly thought of himself as having some special function, some divine commission to speak and act as he did, and in the discharge of that function he went to his death. But to say that he claimed to be the Messiah is quite another matter. If he put some special meaning on that term, that is only to say that in any sense commonly recognised at the time he was not the Messiah. It is perfectly true that the term was understood in various senses. To a Zealot the term Messiah meant some one like a glorified Judas Maccabæus. To a Pharisee it meant above all else a righteous ruler over the people of God set free from heathen oppression. To a pious recluse it might, and perhaps did, mean a superhuman emissary from God. To a Sadducee it probably meant nothing at all. But, while there was thus a considerable range of meaning in which the term Messiah was understood, it is quite evident that Jesus did not identify himself with any of them. And the reason is clear. If he had done so, those who held that particular view of the Messiah would have owned him; and not only so, but if it were really the Messiah which he claimed to be, in whichever of these accepted meanings, then he would be defeating his own ends if he did not openly avow himself such. To claim to be the Messiah, in whatever sense amongst those of which the term allowed in the usage of the time, and still not to act as such would be surely a failure in a clear duty. A supposition which is impossible in the case of Jesus. But, if he believed that the function entrusted to him as a servant of God was not identical with the function of the Messiah in any of its usual meanings, then it is easy to understand the reluctance which he quite plainly showed to admit the application of the term to him, and the obscurity of the language within which his real meaning on the subject lies concealed. If he had not felt that his cause would be endangered by letting himself be identified with any known type of Messiah, his course would have been quite easy. Thus, if he had declared himself to be the Messiah in the Zealot sense he could have had the whole nation at his back in a very short time. If he had declared himself to be the Messiah in the Pharisaic sense, they might indeed have rejected him on the ground that a man who flouted the Halachah and criticised the Torah could not possibly be the Messiah; but at least they would have known where they were. And the claim to be the Messiah was not in itself an offence at all. The tragic hardship of the position of Jesus was that he could not allow his cause and his function to be identified with any of the common expectations of a divine emissary; in some way it was different, doubtless with some sublime grandeur about it known only

to himself, and such that the real understanding of
it perhaps could not be, certainly was not, imparted
to any of his disciples.   To argue, in view of all
this, that he did nevertheless claim to be the Messiah
seems to the present writer to be little more than
futile.

Of course, when Jesus made his first appearance
and began to preach that the kingdom of God was
at hand, there was a stir amongst the people of
Galilee.   And of course the question was asked,
Was this the Messiah ?   And of course an Apocalyptic and Messianic interpretation was put upon
his proclamation of the kingdom and himself as the
herald of it.   That is not remarkable.   What is
remarkable is the fact that so little followed on
Apocalyptic and Messianic lines.   John the Baptist
had proclaimed that the kingdom was at hand.
Crowds flocked to hear him, and then apparently
went away again.   Nothing more was heard of his
movement and only occasional reference to disciples
of John.   It may be said that the movement started
by John was merged in the greater one which began
with Jesus.   No doubt that was so.   But in the
latter case also, the movement, regarded as Apocalyptic and Messianic, came almost to nothing.
Crowds followed Jesus at first, and his fame spread
through all the regions round about.   But the
crowds fell away after a time, as is shown by the
fact that he left Galilee to make a last attempt in
Jerusalem.   If his message had been at all what
the people would expect from an Apocalyptic and
Messianic leader, and what they would have eagerly
accepted, he would have had a host at his back

when he marched on Jerusalem. But when at last he got there, and his handful of followers put on him the appearance of a Messianic triumph (if the story is true) the citizens who watched him asked, Who is this? and the answer was, This is the *prophet* Jesus from Nazareth. The *prophet*, not the Messiah. As an Apocalyptic Messianic demonstration the movement in Galilee had failed; and it failed obviously because Jesus did not and would not give the word which would have resounded through the land. Many were hoping for it, all would have responded to it, and it was never uttered. It was precisely because he would not stoop to the low level of Apocalyptic and betray his trust by announcing himself as the Messiah (knowing what interpretation would be put on his use of the term), that the multitude in Galilee fell away from him, and the crowd in Jerusalem were ready in the space of a week to cry, Crucify him!

The view set forth above as to the relation of Jesus to the function of the Messiah is in harmony with what is told about the close of his life in Jerusalem. There he came into collision with the priesthood and the vested interests of the Temple, and it soon became evident that his death was intended by the authorities. Actually, because a man preaching openly the things that Jesus preached was too dangerous to be allowed his liberty; but ostensibly, because he could be represented as a political offender and handed over to Pilate and the cross. When he was brought to trial before the High Priest it might well be thought that now at last he would declare openly what he was, whether the Messiah or another. Yet the curious uncertainty as to what he really thought hangs over the narrative up to the end. Mark indeed (xiv. 61) says that in answer to the direct question of the High Priest, Art thou the Christ, Jesus gave the direct answer, I am. But Matthew (xxvi. 64) makes him reply, Thou hast said. And Luke (xxii. 70) gives the answer in almost the same terms, Ye say that I am. These are not at all equivalent to the plain affirmative, I am. The form of expression is not common in Hebrew, but there are two clear instances of it, and in both it is implied that the speaker does *not* admit what the questioner means. The sense in the present instance clearly is, " You wish me to own that I am the Messiah. The term is yours not mine. I do not admit it." What Jesus really did mean he did not say, and the writer of Mark is the first of many interpreters who have read into the answer a more definite meaning than it will bear.

Before leaving this question of the alleged Messiahship of Jesus there are one or two points which should be noted from the Jewish side. Merely to claim to be the Messiah was not an offence, neither, as we shall see in the next chapter, was it an offence on the part of one professing to be a Jew to believe that the Messiah had come and that Jesus was he. A century after the death of Jesus another man appeared, Simeon Bar Cocheba, who openly claimed to be the Messiah. He was a Zealot and most of the Pharisaic leaders did not admit his claim. But the greatest of them at the time, Rabbi Akiba, publicly hailed him as the

Messiah. Here was a difference of opinion in regard to an alleged Messiah. No one was brought to trial. Bar Cocheba did not carry the Pharisees with him, with the exception of Akiba, and that pre-eminent teacher was not condemned for his support of Bar Cocheba. He was merely told by one of his colleagues that he would be lying in his grave long before the Son of David really came. Bar Cocheba as a Zealot comes into no near comparison with Jesus, who was certainly not a Zealot. But the two cases turn upon an alleged Messiahship, asserted by some and denied by others; and the inference clearly is that there was nothing mysterious or sacrilegious or criminal in the fact of such a claim being made. Those who say that Judas Iscariot made known to the Chief Priests the deep secret that Jesus was indeed the Messiah, and so betrayed him, make the Chief Priests out to be a good deal more gullible than they probably were. What they wanted was to have Jesus in their power. They needed a betrayer and they bought one. They knew what they meant without the help of Judas to tell them.

One last point in regard to the alleged Messiahship of Jesus is worth considering, especially by those who think that they can bring forth from the obscurity of the Gospel narrative strong evidence that he claimed that title for himself. The Pharisaic literature in what it does say about Jesus is entirely hostile, as can be well understood from what has been said already. And in that literature there is not the slightest reference to any claim put forward either by him or on behalf of him that he was the

Messiah. The point is never mentioned at all in connexion with him, either in the passages which refer specifically to him or in those which deal with controversial encounters between Christians and Jewish teachers in later times. If there had been any ground for charging Jesus with having claimed to be the Messiah, of course from the Pharisaic point of view falsely, the Pharisees would not have failed to have recorded this also against the man who, as they said, " practised magic and deceived and led astray Israel." Of any such charge, even the remotest suggestion of it, neither Talmud nor Midrash contains a single trace. That is the fact, and it is here given for what it is worth. Whatever the Sadducees may have done by way of fastening upon him a charge which they could turn into a political accusation, the Pharisees never raised the question of Messiahship against him.

The first impact of Christianity upon Judaism, in the person of Jesus, is to be found, as already shown, in his repudiation of the Halachah and his criticism of the Torah from the point of view of the free conscience and the prophetic spirit. The second was his attack on the vested interests of the Temple and the priesthood. Of the two, the first was more far-reaching in its effects than the second ; for the first made inevitable the separation of Christianity from Judaism, sooner or later. The second led to the death of Jesus himself, and of course the consequences of that event have been vast and incalculable. But it was not in itself the cause, certainly not the immediate cause, of the separation between Christianity and Judaism. If it had been, then his earliest disciples would not have remained in the Jewish communion, as they certainly did for half a century after his death, and as they tried to do till the time of Jerome and later still. It was the fundamental opposition shown in what I have called the first impact which made the separation inevitable, and showed the attempted compromise of the Jewish Christians to be a hopeless impossibility.

The second impact, the conflict with the priesthood, was in itself (though not in the fatal result to which it led) of much less importance. What was an attack upon the vested interests of a strongly entrenched hierarchy no doubt appeared, in the eyes of the better amongst the priesthood, as an attack upon the ancient and venerable usages and institutions of the established religion. The conflict between Jesus and the priesthood differed in no important respect from the conflict between many a later follower of his and the official authorities of the Church which has taken its name from him and professed to be guided by the Holy Spirit. The Cross is the lineal ancestor of the stake and the gallows; and the Chief Priests, if they ceased to function after the fall of Jerusalem, have had their imitators in Christian Europe. If the act of the official authorities is intelligible in the later instances, and historians have not failed to read its meaning, it is not less intelligible in the earliest instance. And this would be readily admitted if it were not for the unique importance, historical and religious, of the victim.

The death of Jesus marked the end of the first

stage in the process by which Christianity became defined as a separate and different religion from Judaism. There was left, after Jesus was gone, a breach which could not be healed between two widely different conceptions of religion, and a hostility between the respective adherents of those religions which neither side showed any inclination to assuage. What had been, while Jesus lived, distinctive of his own religion became by his death transferred to his followers, in such a way that their religion was no longer centred on an Idea, as Judaism was and continued to be, but was centred on a Person, and that Person Jesus himself. Under every one of its varied phases, in each of its innumerable types, Christianity has always had for its central figure the person of Jesus.

In the next chapter we shall study the process of the separation of Christianity from Judaism, so far as Judaism was affected thereby, the Jewish background of the story told or implied in the New Testament, the Jewish reaction to the Christian movement.

CHAPTER VII

THE SEPARATION OF CHRISTIANITY FROM JUDAISM

THE immediate effect of the death of Jesus was to leave Judaism delivered from its most dangerous enemy. The Pharisees had no longer to fear the unsparing opponent of the Halachah, to whom not even the Torah was above criticism. The Sadducees and the priesthood could feel safe, now that the voice which threatened their privileges was finally silenced. It was true that some followers of Jesus remained, in Jerusalem and presumably in Galilee; but it did not become at once apparent that any danger was to be feared from them. The incidents related in Acts iv.–v. occurred in a time so shortly after the death of Jesus that they can best be regarded as its mere after effects, at all events from the point of view of the leaders of Judaism. " Ye have filled Jerusalem with your teaching, and intend to bring this man's blood upon us " (Acts v. 28). The speech of Gamaliel (*ib.* 34–39), if it is authentic, does not contradict this view. Gamaliel, being a Pharisee, had no liking for the violent measures of the Sadducees, and could see clearly that the surest way to prevent the followers of Jesus from becoming important and perhaps dangerous was to let them alone and take no notice of them. And in fact the danger which

have settled down into a relation to Judaism not markedly different from what it had been before they had known him. It is true, of course, that they believed him to have been the Messiah, while the Jews did not. But this was not after all so important a difference as Christians are apt to think it. While Jesus was alive, indeed, a Jew who believed him to be the Messiah was involved in a movement which might become a revolution, and which in any case carried with it unknown possibilities of far-reaching developments. But after Jesus was dead, and especially after such a death, the belief that he had been the Messiah carried no danger with it; and, if any Jew held that belief, he might hold it if he chose, without running any risk of trouble. What is certain is that the Jewish followers of Jesus did, for the most part, continue in their regular Jewish ways, religious and other. They went up to the Temple (Acts iii. 1) and were in the habit of going there, " day by day " (Acts ii. 46). They went to Synagogue, as they had been accustomed to do, for it was in the Synagogue that the dissensions broke out which led to the death of Stephen (Acts vi. 9). In fact, Jewish Christians were to be found in the Synagogue down to the time of Jerome, early fifth century, and even later. If they had ceased to go there in the very early days of Christianity, they would scarcely have resumed the practice. The trouble all along was that they would go there, in spite of the means taken to detect them, as will be shown presently. In their own eyes they continued to be Jews as much as they had ever been, observing all that the

P

Torah required them to observe, even to the rite of circumcision (Acts xv. 1). The belief that Jesus had been the Messiah lay quite apart from the observance of the Halachah, and was in itself no crime. The case of Akiba and Bar Cocheba mentioned above (p. 217), though it occurred a century later (A.D. 132), gives convincing proof that the mere belief that any given person was the Messiah was no ground for condemnation or even for disapproval. It was a mere difference of opinion; and, from the Jewish point of view, Bar Cocheba was a much more important man than Jesus, judging from the impression he made on his countrymen. To all intents and purposes, the Jewish Christians, at the beginning, were Jews as much as they ever had been, and had no idea that they were adherents of a new religion or that Jesus had founded one. Presumably amongst themselves they hallowed his memory, and included in that memory the remembrance that he had been crucified and slain " by the hand of lawless men " (Acts ii. 23). But they remained in the fellowship of the Synagogue, and, after the disturbances following on the death of Jesus, they were not persecuted. Certainly not for a considerable time, perhaps not at all.

So far, Christianity was merely a special form of Judaism, with no apparent desire or prospect of being anything different. And such on the whole it remained in the belief of the Jewish Christians themselves. It was the admission of Gentile converts into the Christian Church which led to the final separation of the two religions. Paul was not perhaps the first, but he was beyond all comparison the foremost, to preach Christianity to the Gentiles. The Jewish Christians were not unwilling that this should be done; but they could only conceive of such a mission as involving an acceptance of the Torah and the Halachah on the part of the converts. It is remarkable that the most characteristic teaching of Jesus should have left little or no trace in the minds of his Jewish adherents. He would seem to have denounced the Halachah in vain, if his immediate followers made no difficulty of observing it. If they believed him to have been the Messiah, as they did, it was evidently not his teaching which led them to that belief, not even the teaching which was most distinctive of him.

Paul was far more clear-sighted. To him it was evident that in the Christian Church which was to include Gentiles, whether the Jews came in or stayed in or not, there could be no room for the Halachah. Not merely because to require observance of it was out of the question as being a practical impossibility, but also because Christianity itself was in theory incompatible with it. Paul grasped the fact that the Christian religion was founded on a Person, not an Idea. For him, and for the Church after him and ever since, Christ took and kept the place which in Judaism was held and still is held by the Torah. So that for Paul, too, it was not the teaching of Jesus which led him to his belief; and in what he preached as his gospel he laid the whole stress on what Christ had done and on what he was, not on what Jesus had taught. " Christ crucified and risen from the dead " was the keynote of Paul's preaching, and faith in him the watchword of the Church.

From the time, therefore, when Paul began his ministry, a separation of Christianity from Judaism was inevitable; unless, indeed, the one was to prevail over and suppress the other. In any case a period of strife and confusion must be passed through before the relation between Judaism and Christianity could be finally settled and recognised. So far as this definition of the Christian position involved an attack on Judaism it might be regarded as a third impact, in the series of which the first and second were made by Jesus. But the attack on Judaism, so far as there was an attack, was only a necessary factor in the process of separation; and it was separation which Paul saw to be a pressing necessity. The Church must be made independent, free from any embarrassing ties with Judaism, if it was to be able to fulfil its mission. It is curious to observe that Jesus, who said hard things in open attack upon the Halachah, and denounced the Pharisees in unsparing terms, has been in effect far less of an enemy to Judaism than Paul, who professed that his " heart's desire was for Israel that they may be saved " (Rom. x. 1), and whose representation of Judaism is repudiated by every Jew, then and since, as a sheer distortion of the truth.

When Paul went on his missionary journeys, preaching the gospel which was meant for Gentiles as well as for Jews, he seems to have made the local Synagogue his starting-point in every place. The reason for this was that in the Synagogue he would find Jewish hearers who would already know something of what he had to say, and others who were attracted by the Jewish religion (see above, p. 75). He had to begin from Jewish premises, whatever conclusions he might draw from those premises. He had to show that Jesus was the Messiah foretold by the prophets, that in him the promises of the Scriptures were fulfilled, and that the Torah—the Law as he called it—was no longer valid, because Christ replaced it under a higher dispensation. It was true that Gentiles had no ancestral concern with the Torah, and did not need the argument from Scripture; yet even for Gentiles that argument was impressive, since it showed how Christ, of whom they now heard for the first time, had been foreordained in the providence of God, had appeared on earth in the fulness of time, had died and had risen again according to the Scriptures. One would think that Paul could have had but small expectation that Jews would receive with anything but indignant protest the doctrines which he expounded from the Scriptures; and it may be that he only began with Jews so as to give them a chance, if they chose to take it, and that his real e was to gain the Gentile "fearers of God" quented the Synagogues, and through them nce other Gentiles. The scene described xiii. 44–52, in the Synagogue at Antioch ia, may well represent a frequent occurrence l's career as a missionary. "And the next almost the whole city was gathered together the word of God. But when the Jews saw ltitudes, they were filled with jealousy and contradicted the things which were spoken by Paul and blasphemed. And Paul and Barnabas spake out boldly and said, It was necessary that the word of God should first be spoken to you. Seeing ye thrust it from you, and judge yourselves unworthy of eternal life, lo we turn to the Gentiles. For so hath the Lord commanded us, *saying*,

I have set thee for a light of the Gentiles,
That thou shouldest be for salvation unto the uttermost part of the
    earth.

And as the Gentiles heard this, they were glad, and glorified the word of God: and as many as were ordained to eternal life believed. And the word of the Lord was spread abroad throughout all the region. But the Jews urged on the devout women of honourable estate, and the chief men of the city, and stirred up a persecution against Paul and Barnabas, and cast them out of their borders."

The general accuracy of this description will not be questioned by the Christian reader. It will therefore be useful to study it from the Jewish point of view, for the light which it throws upon the process which ended in the final disruption between Judaism and Christianity.

The Gentiles, *i.e.* the non-Jewish frequen[ters of] the Synagogue, were apparently ready to ac[cept the] doctrines of Paul, and with the Gentiles w[as he] concerned. The Jews rejected them. The[ir] position would be this :—We hold the religio[n which] teaches us that God has given the Torah t[o us] as the full revelation of his will and his way[s].

worship and serve him, and walk by the light which he has given. We know, and our fathers have told us, that God is with those who serve him so, who love him with heart and soul and strength and mind. This is what we have learned from our youth up, and this is the strength of our life. Now there comes unto our Synagogue a man who tells us that the Torah is superseded, the revelation made of no effect, except so far as it points to this Jesus, who, we are asked to believe, was the Messiah for whom all Israel has waited.

If the reader has at all grasped the meaning of the teaching given in the Synagogues, as set forth in Chapter III above, he will readily understand how Jews holding such beliefs would resent and indignantly reject the Pauline gospel. It is wholly beside the mark to talk of the obstinacy and stiff-necked opposition of the Jews to a more spiritual truth. The Jews, sincerely believing and holding the religion which is based on Torah, the religion whose inner meaning has been set forth to the best of the writer's ability in the earlier chapters of this book, did not need then, and do not need now, and never have needed, anything that Paul or any other Christian missionary had to offer them. Paul's way of presenting religion might satisfy him, and might be a great improvement on anything which any Gentile had come under Christian influence; Paul's telling him, some d"; and not mere but his own conscience God, made him resolute to " abide in the things that he had learned, knowing from whom he had learned them."

It might have been very much better for the peace of the world if Paul had contented himself with preaching the Gospel to the Gentiles, and had left the Jews alone. But he was in a difficult position, for he could not preach even to the Gentiles without having to explain his attitude to Judaism. The case he had to argue before Gentile hearers was based on the Scriptures, *i.e.* the Old Testament. He had to show that Christ was the fulfilment of the promises made to the fathers, that he was foretold by Moses and the prophets; and it was necessary for the validity of his argument that he should claim divine authority for those Scriptures, as, of course, he would naturally do. But those Scriptures had much to say about the Jews, as the people whom God had chosen, to whom he had given the Torah and sent the prophets. Moreover, those Scriptures were based on the permanence of the religion therein set forth. God had revealed to Israel the truths he held, had directed him to do the things commanded in the Torah, had guided him in setting up the various institutions in and through which he expressed his religion, and all this that Israel might hold a special position in the world and do a special work there, as a perpetual witness to God. These things were the very substance of the Scriptures, and could not be denied if the Scriptures were true.

What, then, was to be done with the very awkward and perplexing fact that the Jews rejected

Christ? The Jews, who were the chosen people of God according to the Scriptures, refused to accept the man whom Paul sought to prove to have been the Messiah according to those same Scriptures. He could not establish his case on the evidence of the Scripture without at the same time discrediting the evidence of those same Scriptures in reference to the divine calling and mission of the Jews. If what he said about Christ was true, that he was foretold in the Scriptures and so forth, and if this was flatly denied by the very people whom God had chosen and by whose prophets and wise men those Scriptures had been written, under divine guidance, then it would seem that God had changed his mind, gone back on his former revelation and set up a new one. If that were really so, then the ancient Scriptures were discredited and their witness was no longer valid; and in that case their evidence in support of Paul's argument for Christ was worthless, and the argument fell to the ground.

This difficulty Paul had to overcome somehow. We may fairly suppose that he looked upon it as an annoying hindrance preventing him from effectively doing his real work as a missionary of Christ. "Woe is me if I preach not the gospel," he said (1 Cor. ix. 16). He was sent to do that, and not to spend his time in study as a theologian or a philosopher. He had to find some way of meeting the objections which thoughtful Gentile "fearers of God" would raise against his argument from the Scriptures. The Jews, he knew well, would not accept it, nor the Christ whom he preached. But the Gentile " fearers of God " whom he met in the Synagogues had some knowledge of the Scriptures and were not Jews; it was these whom he must convince, if he could by any means meet their difficulty. The most elaborate of his attempts in this direction is the Epistle to the Romans. No doubt this was addressed to a community already Christian, but it is evident that many of its intended readers were assumed to have some knowledge of the Jewish religion and the Jewish Scriptures. This would be most naturally accounted for if the readers in question had been Gentile " fearers of God," who had previously been associated with some Synagogue. Jews who remained steadfast in their Judaism would not be found in a community of Christians, and, if addressed to them, the Epistle to the Romans would have other than the desired effect. In chapter xi. Paul puts forward his theory to account for the rejection of Christ by the Jews, and also to meet the objection raised against the self-contradiction of the Scriptures. The theory, of course, is that " a hardening in part hath befallen Israel, until the fulness of the Gentiles be come in, and so all Israel shall be saved. . . . As touching the gospel, they are enemies for your sake; but as touching the election they are beloved for the fathers' sake. For the gifts and the calling of God are without repentance. For as ye in time past were disobedient to God, but now have obtained mercy by their disobedience, even so have these also now been disobedient that by the mercy shown to you they also may now obtain mercy. For God hath shut up all unto disobedience that he might have mercy upon all."

The argument worked out in the Epistle to the Romans only has any pretence to validity if the premisses from which it starts are granted. And one of these premisses was that Judaism, as a religion, was marked by certain characteristic defects. The Torah, which is represented throughout as Law, is alleged to have been given " that the trespass might abound " (Rom. v. 20); and although it is spoken of as holy, and the Commandment holy (vii. 12), yet it is regarded as ineffective for salvation. Its real effect is to bring about a state of universal sin from which the only deliverance is through faith in Christ. Such an argument could only have weight with readers who had no intimate knowledge of Judaism—men like the " fearers of God " who had been attracted to the Synagogue but had not grown up there. To the real Jew the argument is entirely worthless, because it involves a conception of Judaism which is not in accordance with the facts, both historical facts and convictions of truth in the Jewish consciousness. Judaism such as Paul depicted it has never existed outside his own imagination; and all Jewish literature and, what is more, Jewish life ever since his day bears witness to the falseness of his representation of it. If, as there is no reason to doubt since he says it himself, he was born and bred a Jew, and even a Pharisee, one can only marvel at the mental transformation whereby he became so possessed by the thought of Christ that he became unable to recognise, or found himself driven to ignore, that which lay at the heart of the Judaism he had left, and which made it then, and makes it still, God's own truth to those who have remained faithful to it.

Paul's theory, weak and mischievous as it is and from the Jewish point of view entirely false, is nevertheless not to be regarded as an attack on Judaism. It was a rather desperate makeshift to get free from Judaism, to set the Christian Church at liberty from the entanglement of its Jewish origin. To do that was necessary if the Christian religion was to be taken out into the Gentile world in such a form that Gentiles, who had no previous association with Jews, could receive it. Paul may have been so carried away with enthusiasm for his gospel that he did not realise all that he was doing; or he may have thought that in view of his supreme object—to make Christ known to the Gentiles—it did not greatly matter what the Jews thought, since they had rejected Christ; or that since the Christian Church must be torn away from the Jewish connexion, if it was to live at all, some amount of pain in the process was unavoidable, and those who were made to suffer must bear it as well as they could. Whatever the explanation be, the fact remains that the separation of Christianity from Judaism, which was very largely due to Paul, was effected by sheer perversion of the truth. And the Christian Church has complacently accepted that perversion of the truth ever since.

Nor was this the whole of the wrong which was done to Judaism in the process of separation. The claim was made at a very early period that Christians were the true Israel, the rightful heirs of the promises in the Old Testament Scriptures. Paul led the way to this conception, when he declared (Rom. ix. 6–8), " For they are not all Israel which are of Israel ; neither, because they are Abraham's seed are they all children ; but, In Isaac shall thy seed be called. That is, it is not the children of the flesh that are children of God, but the children of the promise are reckoned for a seed." In itself this fantastic distinction was of no great importance ; but it helped to develop, if it did not actually give rise to, the idea that the Christian Church had stepped into the place of the Jewish community, henceforth to enjoy all the privileges bestowed upon Israel according to the Scriptures. Those Scriptures themselves, which had already been interpreted in a Christian sense, were claimed as the rightful property of the Church against those whose inheritance they were. If any doubt existed in Christian minds as to the validity or the honesty of this claim, a powerful argument in its favour was provided by the disastrous war which ended in the capture of Jerusalem by the Romans and the destruction of the Temple, A.D. 70. Could there be a plainer proof that God had done with the Jews and thrown them over, doubtless because they had rejected Christ and put him to death ? The Church did not remain content with the theory of Paul, which left the door open for an eventual bringing in of the Jews, when they should have recovered from their temporary " hardening." The Church took the position, and never abandoned it, that the whole dispensation set forth in the Old Testament was at an end, that Christ had abolished the Law, that Israel had forfeited his position as the chosen people of God, and that the Church was his rightful successor for all purposes.

Christians are so accustomed to this conception, that they seldom realise that it is entirely without any foundation, either in historical fact or in moral right. As a matter of history Judaism has never been superseded and has remained in full vitality as a religion from that day to this. Considered from the point of view of moral right, the Christian appropriation of the Scriptures, the status, the very name of Israel, is a sheer act of usurpation, an outrage inflicted upon Judaism, amongst the most deadly of the long series of wrongs which Jews have suffered through the centuries at the hands of the Christian Church.

When the Christian gospel was preached in the Synagogues, by Paul and others who followed in his steps, Jews who were present had to listen to such arguments as those we have been considering, all tending to show that Judaism was an inferior religion and had outlived its right of existence. It is not wonderful that they protested; and, if there is any duty of being true to conviction, it was clearly right that they should protest. In the description quoted above (p. 229) of the disturbance in Antioch of Pisidia (Acts xiii. 44–52), it is said that the Jews " blasphemed " (ver. 45) and that they " stirred up a persecution " against Paul and Barnabas. That is how it appeared from the Christian side. Any candid reader who will take the trouble to realise what it meant to Jews will

see that the " blasphemy " was righteous indignation, and the " persecution " a just effort of self-
defence.   Are not even Christian bishops and clergy-
men made to promise that they will drive away
strange doctrine ? If the early preachers of the
gospel thought it their duty to flout the deep and
sincere convictions of Jewish hearers wherever they
came, they were not entitled to complain of the
opposition which they provoked ; and to speak of
" blasphemy " and " persecution " is an abuse of
terms, however natural such terms might seem to
the " New Israel " that stooped to make use of
them.

By such methods, amongst others, the gospel
made its way ; and wherever it came it stirred up
strife and left anger and pain and powerless indignation in Jewish hearts. The Christian reader of
the New Testament knows little about these things,
and is regaled with a pleasing picture of how the
true faith was spread by brave men and devoted
missionaries. So it was, and what the New Testament testifies in this respect is in the main true.
But the New Testament does not give the other
side of the picture. If it did, Christian readers
would not be so ready to wonder at the stubborn
refusal of Jews, both then and since, to have anything to do with the Christian gospel.

All this was part of the process of tearing loose
the Christian Church from Judaism ; and, so far
as it resulted in conversions to Christianity, Judaism
was no further affected than by the pain inflicted.
What the churches, whose members were acquired
by these means, chose to do as Christians was their

own affair. If they had been Jews, they were lost to Judaism. If they had been Gentiles, they were of no concern to the Synagogue. But we have already seen that the earliest followers of Jesus remained closely associated with the Jewish community, remained indeed within that community, being in every respect but one conforming Jews. They believed Jesus to have been the Messiah; otherwise they were as other Jews. They were to be found in the Synagogues, and, while it still stood, in the Temple. And for a while no trouble ensued, no objection was raised against them for doing so. Merely because no reason would present itself for any such objection. And so it might have remained, and very probably would have remained, if the Christian movement had not made rapid progress amongst the Gentiles, through such preaching as has been indicated above. The admission of Gentile converts into the Church began to disturb the harmony and to bring in new problems.

One result of the admission of Gentiles into the Church, or perhaps to some extent a cause of it, was a change in the way in which the person of Christ was regarded. The original simplicity of the man of Nazareth was no longer found to be sufficient, not even as prophet, not even as Messiah. The Christ who appears in the Epistles of Paul is not so much a human as a cosmic being; and though Paul never in so many words called him God, yet he had advanced a long way beyond the position that Jesus was just a man, like other men. Teaching of this kind rapidly took a foremost place in Christian theology. No doubt it was developed chiefly and most rapidly amongst Gentile Christians, in centres outside Palestine. But sooner or later it was bound to make its influence felt in Jewish Christian communities such as have already been mentioned; and, beyond any question, it found some measure of acceptance there. The Epistle to the Hebrews is evidence that this was really the case. It is generally agreed that this epistle was addressed to Jewish Christians, though it is not certain which was the particular community of them which the writer had in view. There is indeed no proof that the Epistle to the Hebrews was known and read in Palestine, but it seems reasonable to suppose that Jewish Christians there would hold some such views, and be open to such persuasion, as Jewish Christians in other places.

Here then we have a new feature making its appearance in the belief and teaching of Jewish Christians; and it consisted in this, that Christ was regarded as a being almost if not quite identified with God, such a one that the term Son of God when applied to him carried a meaning higher and greater than it could have in any other connexion— " His Son, whom he appointed heir of all things, through whom also he made the worlds; who being the effulgence of his glory and the very image of his substance, upholding all things by the word of his power," etc. (Heb. i. 2, 3). The obvious effect of such new teaching as this was very seriously to disturb the harmony between Jewish Christianity and the parent Judaism. Up till this time it was possible to combine a belief in Jesus as the Messiah with a strict observance of all the practical precepts

Q

of Judaism, and a sincere belief in the Sole Unity
of God, and thus to remain within the community
of Israel without incurring any censure. But it
was not possible to combine with loyalty to Jewish
beliefs and principles the acceptance of a doctrine
which raised Christ almost if not quite to the level
of God. For to assert this was to infringe the
divine Unity, the very corner-stone of Judaism;
and, if this was asserted, if this doctrine was held
and presumably taught by men who still professed
to be Jews, still attended the Synagogue, still
observed the precepts, etc., then Judaism was
exposed to grave danger, all the more formidable
because it was concealed under an outward appearance of loyal profession. The Jewish Christians
holding this doctrine were an enemy within the
gates, traitors in the camp, and no terms could be
made with them if Judaism was to survive.

The situation here indicated corresponds point
for point with that which is disclosed in the Rabbinical literature in reference to certain persons
called Mīnīm. The word Min denotes a Jewish
sectary of some kind, and it certainly includes
Jewish Christians, as we have seen in the story of
Rabbi Eliezer referred to above (see p. 191). The
Minim are referred to as deadly enemies of Judaism,
all the more formidable because they were secret,
hiding themselves under the profession of loyal
observance. They were, or they might be, present
in any Synagogue. A Min might even recite the
prayers. Most of the references to the Minim
belong to the latter half of the first century and
the greater part of the second, and the situation

implied in them is to be found in Palestine. Many of the passages, especially those of the second century, describe controversial encounters between a Min and a Rabbi. And one very important group of passages has to do with an official measure of protection against the Minim, introduced by the authority of Gamaliel II, grandson of the Gamaliel of Acts v. 34.

It would be impossible to present the case in reference to the Minim without an amount of reference to Rabbinical passages far beyond the scope of this book. The reader who wishes to know more about them is referred to the complete study of them mentioned below.* One or two points, however, may be usefully mentioned here. It would be hard to express with more bitter emphasis than is done in some of the Rabbinical passages the horror which was felt towards the Minim by the leading Jewish teachers. They serve to show that the danger feared from the side of the Minim was very great, greater than that which the ordinary Gentile idolater could bring about. The Gentile, so far as his example and his practice were offensive to the Jewish mind, was a long-familiar danger, and no concealment of it was possible or to be thought of. The Jewish community lived in the midst of Gentiles, and had done so for centuries. The Gentile influence, for good or for evil, was well known, and the way of counteracting that influence was a matter of long-

* For a collection of the Minim passages in the Rabbinical literature, translated and explained, see my *Christianity in Talmud and Midrash*, where they fill the second half of the book.

settled policy. Since the time of the Maccabees, there was no particular occasion on which it was found necessary to devise special precautions against the influence of the ordinary Gentile.

But in the case of the Minim it was found necessary to take special precautions; and the time at which this was done can be determined within limits which are fairly close. Somewhere about the year A.D. 80 a significant addition was made to the daily prayers, by the insertion of a clause which ran thus: " May there be no hope for the Minim." This is what is usually known as the Formula against the Minim (Birchath ha-Minim, *i.e.* literally, the blessing of the Minim). Now this formula was not so much a measure of defence as a means of detection. The words in which it was expressed were such that no one, if he were himself a Min, could honestly recite them. He would be condemning himself, and inviting the congregation to confirm that condemnation by saying Amen at the end of the clause. If he left the words out he would at once betray himself as a Min. It is recorded that the author of the formula, a certain revered teacher known as Samuel the Small, on one occasion himself forgot the words as he was reciting the prayers; and the congregation in the Synagogue waited for two and even for three hours rather than call him from the desk, in order to let him have the chance to recall the words to mind. They did this because he was a man greatly respected and, as I believe, very old, and they did not wish to put him to open shame. But, if it had been any one else, the inference would have been drawn that he was a Min.

The formula is still to be found in the Jewish prayer book, but as read now it does not contain the word Minim. The word used is Malshinim, the slanderers. But it is referred to as the Birchath ha-Minim in very early texts, and there can be no reasonable doubt as to the word. Some scholars have supposed that the original word was Nōtzrim, *i.e.* Nazarenes; but there is no proof of this. But there can be no doubt that the formula was directed against Jewish Christians, and this would be enough to account for the assertion made by early Christian writers, that the Jews were accustomed to curse the Christians three times a day in their prayers.

It is evident that the formula against the Minim could do nothing to meet the actual danger arising out of false teaching on their part. That could only be done by argument, as is shown by the numerous polemical discussions mentioned in the Rabbinical literature. But the formula served or was intended to unmask a concealed enemy and bring him out into the open. It was a method of showing " who was on the Lord's side," and who was not. Yet even so, it seems rather ineffectual, or at all events very limited in its range. It would only act in the case of the man who recited the prayers. The rest of the congregation would not be implicated, since they were not reciting ; or, if they were, this or that man who remained silent in this particular passage could easily pass unnoticed among the rest. No case is recorded of any one being actually detected as a Min by the help of this formula. But the point of chief importance is this, that a precaution was officially adopted, about the time already mentioned, and that no such precaution was taken in regard to any other class of offenders or suspects.

The close correspondence between the Minim of the Talmud and the Jewish Christians may be followed still further. It has been shown above that the original simplicity of the belief in Jesus as the Messiah was replaced by a doctrine of Christ which tended to raise him almost if not quite to the level of God. This new feature made its influence felt towards the close of the first century, and it was in that same period that the official precaution was taken by the adoption of the formula against the Minim. It is at and after this time that most of the polemical encounters took place in which the Rabbis met the attacks of the Minim; and what has been said in reference to the change in the Christology of the Jewish Christians explains why it was that neither on the one side nor on the other was the question of the Messiahship of Jesus ever raised. That did not matter in face of the much more serious assertion that he was in some sense practically on a level with God. In these polemical encounters the question most often in dispute was whether there were two powers in heaven. The doctrine of the Two Powers is specifically connected with the Minim; and to identify the Minim on this account with the Gnostics is to go off on a false scent. The point cannot be discussed here.

The Jewish Christians represent the only side of

the Christian Church with which Judaism had any close contact. The Gentile Church, which included the large and growing majority of Christians, tore itself loose and left Judaism for ever. The Jewish Christian minority showed no inclination to sever the connexion with the Synagogue, and in fact never did so. But the severance was accomplished by the official measure of the formula against the Minim, which implied that Judaism would no longer recognise the Jewish Christians as having any rightful place in the community of Israel. They might continue to occupy that place, but they were regarded as secret and dangerous enemies. The time came, indeed, when it was evident that the Jewish Christians could do no harm to Judaism, being themselves repudiated as heretics by the official Christian Church. So they were left to themselves, and the community of Israel ceased to take much notice of them. They had tried to face both ways; as Jerome rather unkindly said of them, they professed to be both Jews and Christians, while in fact they were neither Jews nor Christians. So they remained a dwindling remnant under the name of Nazarenes or Ebionites (in Christian usage) or Minim in the Talmud and Midrash, until they died out and dropped into the limbo of forgotten things.

The decisive separation of Christianity from Judaism was practically completed by the end of the first century; and each of the two went on its way, never again to meet in any kind of fellowship. What Christianity became is writ large in the pages of history. Judaism kept fast hold of what it had for ages held sacred, the Torah and the belief in the Divine Unity, and what these meant for Judaism it has been the object of this book to show. And the passionate conviction with which it held to the revelation it had received was only strengthened by the assaults which had been made upon it, in the name, and by the preachers of the new religion. Judaism, throughout the century which saw the rise of Christianity, had occasion to know what was meant by the saying " Blessed are ye when men shall reproach you . . . and say all manner of evil against you falsely " (Matt. v. 11). The Christian Church, beginning with its founder, at least put Judaism in the way of finding that particular blessing. And perhaps Judaism at the end of the New Testament period was in some respects ennobled and exalted by all that it had gone through during that time. Not indeed that Christianity had made much impression on it, so as to bring about any considerable change, or any change at all, in its belief or its practices. While the process of separation was going on, Judaism suffered annoyance and pain and many a smarting wound ; but, when that was over, Judaism remained in unimpaired strength and vitality as a living religion. Far more serious than the separation of Christianity was the national disaster of the war which ended with the fall of Jerusalem and the destruction of the Temple, A.D. 70. Yet the effect of this was to leave the strongest element in Judaism, the religion of the Pharisees, in possession of the field so to speak. The Sadducees were gone, the Zealots were exhausted. The Pharisees were the only ones left who could or did step into the breach and save what could be saved

out of the wreck. And the defeat of the last
desperate revolt against Rome, the war of Bar
Cocheba, A.D. 132–135, only emphasised the same
truth. Judaism as a religion had twice been tried
in the furnace, and the result was to purge away
the dross and leave the finer metal. So, far from
being superseded, her divine Torah replaced by the
gospel, or any of the things so confidently asserted
by those who do not know her well, she went forward along the way appointed for her with a deeper
conviction of the truth committed to her, a more
resolute trust in God who had given her her hard
and dangerous task, and a more passionate resolve
to be faithful unto death in that sublime service.

There had been a parting of the ways, a choice
to be made, when the Christian gospel was offered
to her. She made her choice, and has remained
faithful to it. What was offered her she needed
not; she had her own way of thinking about God,
serving him, trusting him, living and dying for him.
The gospel might indeed be a light to the Gentiles,
and if so, the blessing of God would go with it;
but he had spoken to Israel, and Israel had hearkened
to him, and until the Torah had ceased to be his
divine word, Israel would have no other. And so
it has remained. The Christian Church, which has
marched forward to victory over the pagan world,
and celebrated in every land the triumph of the
Cross, seldom reflects upon and still more seldom
understands the meaning of what she did in the
early years of her existence as it affected the Judaism
in whose midst she was born. She can at least
find there a new application of words which her

chief apostle taught her: "Pressed on every side yet not straitened, perplexed yet not unto despair, pursued yet not forsaken, smitten down yet not destroyed." Such has been the fate of Judaism, through the mournful and cruel centuries. And its watchword has ever been: "Though he slay me, yet will I trust in him."

GENERAL INDEX

A

Abraham, 17
Adam, 105
Akiba, Rabbi, 191, 217, 226
Am ha-aretz, 59, 72–4, 131–8,
    195
Ananias (High Priest), 145
Angels, 91
Annas, 145
Antiochus Epiphanes, 37, 45,
    59
Apocalyptic literature, 10, 11,
    61, 81, 111, 123–33, 212
Asceticism, 63–4, 93
Assideans, 45

B

Bar Cocheba, 12, 79, 217, 226,
    249
Beth Din, 153, 154, 155, 171

C

Caiaphas, 145
Captain, of Temple, 145
Captivity (see Exile).
Chamber of the Silent, 150
Circumcision, 19, 174, 176
" Common ground " between
    Jesus and the Pharisees, 187–
    203
Corban, 208

Covenant, 17, 97
Council (see Sanhedrin).

D

Devils, 91
Diaspora, 40, 126, 172
Dietary laws, 174
Doctors of the law, 155

E

Eliezer, Rabbi, 191
Essenes, 61, 62–5, 93, 118–20
Exile, the, 15, 16, 21, 178
Ezekiel, 21, 33, 113
Ezra, 21, 26, 32, 34–6, 41, 124

F

" Father in Heaven," 88–90,
    188
Fearers of God, 75, 173, 229,
    233
Festivals, attendance at, 147–8

G

Gamaliel I, 155, 222
—— II, 168
Gehenna, 117
Gezeroth (see Ordinances).
God, belief, 16, 87–92
—— character of, 18

God, names for, 90
—— of Israel, 17
—— Unity of, 91

H

Hadrian, 12
Haggadah, 56–8, 83–4, 124, 128, 193
Halachah, 54–8, 83, 86, 99, 123, 128, 156, 175, 179–82, 205, 207
Hasidim, 45, 124
Hazan (*see* Minister).
Herod the Great, 27, 61
Herodians, 71
Hezekiah (" robber chieftain "), 66.
Hillel, 70, 160
Hypocrisy, 55

I

Idolatry, 16
Immortality, 19, 115
Individual, the, in post-Exilic Judaism, 20–2, 32, 33
Interpretation of the Torah, 51–3
Israel, relation of, to God, 17, 96–8

J

Jesus, 74, 185 fol. (and Chap. VI *passim*)
Jewish Christians, 225–7 (and *see* Minim).
John the Baptist, 111, 215
Josephus, 10, 11, 66, 73, 148
Judas Iscariot, 70, 218
—— of Galilee, 66, 67, 70

K

Kannai (*see* Zealots).
Kingdom of God (Heaven), 105–9, 212

L

Law (*see* Torah).

M

Maccabeans, the 37, 45, 59, 67
Man, nature of, 92–5
Marriages, mixed, 34
Mattathias, 67
Memra, 91
Merit, 101
Messiah, the, 19, 69, 109–13, 211–19
Midrash(im), 82, 83, 190
Min(im), 191, 242–7
Minhag, 177
Minister, 165–6
Mitzvah, 99
Moses, 17

N

Names of God, 90
Nehemiah, 36, 43

O

Ordinances, 42, 43

P

Paul, 31, 95, 103, 158, 170, 173, 224, 226 (and onwards *passim*)
Pharisees, 12, 46–7 (and *passim*)
Prayer, 98
Priest, High, 144–5
Priests, Chief, 144–5, 218, 220
Proselytes, 74–6
—— of the gate, 75

R

Rabbi (title), 157
Rabbinical literature, 11–12, 82–4
Repentance, 102–3
Resurrection, 19, 112–7
Revelation, 96–7
Reward, 19, 100

S

Sabbath, the, 19, 136, 174
Sacrifices, animal, 142–3
Sadducees, 47, 48–50, 120–3 (and *passim*)
Sanhedrin, 152–5
Scribe(s), 36, 157, 158, 159
Sermon, 169–70
Shammai, 70, 160
Shechinah, 91
Shekel, the half, 141
Shema, the, 107, 168
Sicarii, 68
Silent, Chamber of the, 150
Sin, 102–5
—— unpardonable, the alleged, 103
Synagogue, the, 25–30, 73, 133–8, 161–73

Synagogue, relation in the Temple, 27–30
—— Ruler of, 165
—— service, 166–71
—— the Great, 37

T

Temple, the, 12, 16, 19, 27, 134, 140–51, 210, 224
Torah, 21, 30–2 (and *passim*)
Tradition, oral, 44
—— of the Elders, 55, 200
Tribute money, 161
" Trumpets," the, 150–1

U

Unity of God, 91

V

Vespasian, 12

Y

Yetzers, the two, 94–5

Z

Zealots, 65–71, 77–8, 111, 118, 131–3, 204

INDEX OF OLD TESTAMENT PASSAGES CITED

Exodus

xx. 10 75

Numbers

xv. 37–41 167

Deuteronomy

vi. 4, 5 . . . 106, 107
vii. 3 34
xi. 13–21 167
xvii. 9–11 42

Nehemiah

viii. 8 52
ix. x 36, 43

Psalms

cxlv. 13 107

Isaiah

xi. 9 108
xliii. 10–15 196
lvii. 15 88

Jeremiah

xxxi. 29 22

1 Maccabees

ii. 27 67
45–8 68

INDEX OF NEW TESTAMENT PASSAGES CITED

Matt.

v. 11	248
43	198
vi. 2	151
ix. 11	200
36	137
x. 17	154, 171
xi. 12	70
xii. 2	200
xv. 2	200
xvii. 24–7	141
xx. 18	159
xxi. 14	150
xxii. 15	161
16	71
xxiii.	206
2	159
6	164
15	75
23	56
xxv. 31	116
xxvi. 30	166
55	150
64	217

Mark

i. 14	186
21	186
22	198
32	186

Mark

i. 39	186
ii. 7	103
16	159, 160
23	205
iii. 1	205
18	70
22	204
vi. 34	74, 195
vii. 1	206
3	54, 175
9	206
viii. 15	71
x. 2	206
xii. 13	71, 206
29, 30	107
41–4	150
xiv. 49	170
53	154
61	217

Luke

ii.	145, 189
iii. 2	145
iv. 16, 20	163, 164, 166, 167, 193
v. 17	159
x. 25	160
xiii. 14	165
xiv. 1	159

Luke

xviii. 10 149
xviii. 11, 12 98
xxii. 66 159
    70 217
xxiii. 50 . . . 155, 160

John

vii. 37 177
xviii. 13, 24 145

Acts

ii. 23 226
    46 225
iii. 1, 2, 10, 11 . 149, 225
iv. 222
    6 145
v. 222
    28 222
    34–9 222
    34 155
    37 70
vi. 9 . . . 172, 225
ix. 2 223
xiii. 15, 16 . . 165, 170
    16 75
    44–52 . . 229, 238

Acts

xiv. 1 173
xv. 1 226
xviii. 8, 17 173
xxi. 28 150
    31 145
xxiii. 9 160

Romans

v. 20 235
vii. 95
    12 235
ix. 6–8 237
x. 1 228
xi. 234

1 Corinthians

ix. 16 233

Galatians

v. 17 95

Hebrews

i. 2–3 241

James

i. 14 94